PITTSBURGH *AND THE* GREAT MIGRATION

PITTSBURGH *AND THE* GREAT MIGRATION

······························

Black Mobility and the Automobile

THE
FRICK PITTSBURGH

COMPILED BY KIM CADY

THE
History
PRESS

Published by The History Press
Charleston, SC
www.historypress.com

Cover image: Barbara Jones posed next to a car on Mulford Street, Homewood, Pittsburgh, Pennsylvania, circa 1937. *Carnegie Museum of Art, Pittsburgh, Heinz Family Fund, Charles "Teenie" Harris Archive, 2001.35.8275.*

First published 2023

Manufactured in the United States

ISBN 9781467153140

Library of Congress Control Number: 2022948309

Arts, Equity, & Education Fund celebrates diverse voices in the arts. Through underwriting publications such as *Pittsburgh and the Great Migration: Black Mobility and the Automobile*, AE&E Fund helps create lasting documentation that inspires scholarship and future generations of art enthusiasts.

CONTENTS

FOREWORD

The Wylie Avenue jazz scene. The Pittsburgh Crawfords Negro National League baseball team. The photojournalism of Teenie Harris. The plays of August Wilson. From the 1930s, Pittsburgh rose to become a vibrant center of African American culture. Why here? Why then? This volume traces part of the answer by exploring the role of the automobile in the Great Migration to Pittsburgh, in which Black Americans moved from the South to this northern city for the promise of industrial jobs and a better life.

Like all important projects, this book is the result of many contributions. Its conception—like the idea for the compelling exhibition that it accompanies—is due to Kimberly Cady, associate curator, Car and Carriage Museum, the Frick Pittsburgh. For assembling a dream team of contributors and advisors—Ron Baraff, Samuel W. Black, Charlene Foggie-Barnett, Laurence A. Glasco, Jonnet Solomon, Gretchen Sullivan Sorin, Joe William Trotter Jr. and Mark Whitaker—and for stewarding the project to its successful completion, we owe her a debt of gratitude.

This volume is the first publication ever created in conjunction with an exhibition in the Car and Carriage Museum. But it is surely not the last. All of us at the Frick are deeply grateful to the Arts, Equity, & Education Fund for first sparking the idea that we might create this book and for the very generous support that has made its publication possible.

Thank you, all.

—Elizabeth E. Barker
Executive Director, Frick Pittsburgh

INTRODUCTION

Like most people, I have this sort of love-hate relationship with Pittsburgh. This is my home, and at times I miss it and find it tremendously exciting, and other times I want to catch the first thing out that has wheels.
—August Wilson, playwright

Buying a car is one of the first steps many take as they transition into the middle class, but for Black car owners, this step was more than just a symbol of "making it." Automobile ownership provided a real sense of freedom. It was freedom from the remembered restraints of slavery, from timetables of trains and buses and, most importantly, freedom of unrestricted mobility, the ability to come and go as one pleases.

After the emancipation of enslaved people in the 1870s, the Reconstructionist government of the South enacted and enforced laws that segregated and continued the subjugation of newly freed Blacks. Once free, they continued to face traveling restrictions in segregated public transportation. Those who dared to challenge these laws faced, at best, humiliation and, at worst, death at the hands of angry white passengers, drivers and law enforcement. Accessibility to private transportation lessened the harassment and physical dangers Black people endured on public transit. It also provided a sense of independence and freedom of mobility that had only been privy to white people.

Pittsburgh and the Great Migration: Black Mobility and the Automobile examines an era in our history that many ignore: the period after the Civil War and

A fleet of Pontiac Streamliners, circa 1940–46, at the Owl Cab Company located in Pittsburgh's Hill District. *Charles "Teenie" Harris Archive/Carnegie Museum of Art via Getty Images.*

before civil rights. The exhibition focuses on automobile ownership and its effect on Black lives during the Great Migration—when two million African Americans left the South, seeking a better quality of life.

Those with the means packed what they could fit in a suitcase and left their homes and families behind. Searching for better opportunities, they traveled to the budding industries of the North and Midwest while escaping discriminatory laws and racial violence in the South. They would travel to areas where family before them had settled and recreate their familiar lives in these foreign places upon arrival. Cities like Detroit, Chicago, Cleveland and Pittsburgh—whose Black population doubled between 1916 and 1930—provided the setting for the storied journeys of many migrants.

Pittsburgh and the Great Migration explores the strong Black communities thriving in Pittsburgh during this period, which attracted migrants from Alabama and Virginia. Charles "Teenie" Harris, the photographer for the Black-owned *Pittsburgh Courier,* mobilized would-be migrants with his depiction of life in Pittsburgh as a prominent stop on the Northeast jazz

The Streamliner "Torpedo Fleet" established Pontiac's dominance above the "big three": Chevrolet, Ford, Plymouth. *Courtesy The NB Center for American Automotive Heritage.*

circuit, with clubs like the Crawford Grill and the Hurricane Club. Poet Claude McKay referred to the Hill District neighborhood as the "Crossroads of the World." The numerous businesses established out of necessity to combat discrimination exemplify Black Pittsburgh's entrepreneurial spirit. The National Negro Opera House in Homewood was devoted to providing a space for Black musicians to study and prosper. The Owl Cab Company served the Black residents of the Hill and surrounding communities when white-owned car services refused. *Pittsburgh and the Great Migration* explores how neighborhoods like the Hill District expanded and changed with the influx of southern Blacks and the role the automobile and transportation played in this transformation.

—Kimberly Cady
Associate Curator, Car and Carriage Museum

ACKNOWLEDGEMENTS

I am fortunate to work for an institution that allows me to take the wheel in developing unique exhibitions with its historic transportation collection. This autonomy has permitted me to focus on the social history of the automobile and its effect on everyday life. *Pittsburgh and the Great Migration: Black Mobility and the Automobile* is a continuation of that social history focus, looking at the role the automobile played in furthering African American freedom. Researching and developing this exhibition and the accompanying catalogue has been more rewarding than I imagined. It was a privilege to work with an extraordinary team of writers to highlight the strides of Pittsburgh's Black communities while not diminishing the real struggles faced by those who ventured to the region. While this exhibition and catalogue certainly cannot address all the highs or struggles of Black mobility, I hope they provide an opportunity for reflection and discussion.

In addition to the support of Elizabeth Barker, executive director, and Dawn Brean, chief curator and director of collections at the Frick Pittsburgh, this catalogue would not have been possible without the financial support of the Arts, Equity, & Education Fund. I'm grateful for the AE&E's recognition of my work on previous exhibitions and, having faith in my convictions, choosing to underwrite the *Pittsburgh and the Great Migration* catalogue. I sincerely thank the authors who wholeheartedly accepted my offer to contribute to the publication; each of their revealing and informative essays has created an illuminating read. Many thanks to my extraordinary advisory panel composed of Pittsburgh historians and academics, many of whom contributed essays to this publication. Your guidance and direction were instrumental in synthesizing the scope and themes of the exhibition and accompanying catalogue.

I am thankful to lenders who enthusiastically chose to be part of this endeavor: the Henry Ford in Dearborn, Michigan; the NB Center for American Automotive Heritage in Allentown, Pennsylvania; the Auburn Cord Duesenberg Automobile Museum in Auburn, Indiana; the Western Reserve Historical Society in Cleveland, Ohio; and the GM Heritage Center in Sterling Heights, Michigan.

Many thanks to Mary Seelhorst, editor, and our anonymous peer reviewer for their insights and patience during the multiple rounds of reviews and edits. I'm grateful to my curatorial colleagues, Melanie Groves, registrar and manager of exhibitions, and Morgan Lawrence, collections and exhibitions assistant, for bearing the weight of other curatorial projects while I worked to meet publication and exhibition deadlines. Lastly, I am forever indebted to Alonna Carter-Donaldson, publications assistant, who kept everything on course. This catalogue would not have been possible without her fantastic work ethic, dedication, understanding and numerous late-night emails; I am so thankful for you.

—Kimberly Cady

Chapter 1

MOBILITY

A Fundamental Right

by Gretchen Sullivan Sorin, Director and Distinguished Service Professor at the Cooperstown Graduate Program, State University of New York at Oneonta

I n 1857, Austin Steward wrote the story of his life and his path to freedom as an enslaved person. In his memoir, *Twenty-Two Years a Slave and Forty Years a Freeman*, he recounted the harsh punishment that might be meted out to a slave for being caught away from the master's property without a pass. "Slaves are never allowed to leave the plantation to which they belong without a pass," wrote Steward. "Should any one venture to disobey this law, he will most likely be caught by the patrol and given thirty-nine lashes."[1] These slave passes—small handwritten slips of paper or in some cases metal tags pinned to one's clothing—represented power. Slave masters used them as a method of racial control. Even an enslaved person who sought to visit family members on nearby plantations might be punished if found without written permission from his owner. The mobility of enslaved persons was strictly controlled to ensure that they did not run away or gather clandestinely at night to foment rebellion against their masters. The requirement to have a pass, and the punishment handed out if found without one, also reinforced the idea that an enslaved person had no right to control her own movements or make her own decisions.

From the moment the first Africans stepped ashore in the New World, they faced a life of restricted mobility. Cities passed laws prohibiting Black people from gathering or requiring that they get permits or licenses for community events, to own firearms or to open businesses—requirements not set for people who were not Black. Yet the freedom of mobility, the right to move about as one pleased has always been a central aspect of American freedom. As the Continental Congress prepared to establish a constitutional government from thirteen disparate colonies, a committee composed of one representative from each colony gathered to devise an agreement that outlined how the colonies would operate as a new nation. The "Articles of Confederation and Perpetual Union" provided the structure for the new government. Ratified by all thirteen states by 1781 and in effect until 1789, when it was replaced by the Constitution of the United States, the document clearly addressed the importance of the freedom of movement. Article four noted, "The people of each state shall have free ingress and regress to and from any other state, and shall enjoy therein all the privileges of trade and commerce." The ongoing weakness of the new government and the economic, political and structural problems that plagued such a loose confederation of states led to the need for a new constitution. The concept of freedom of movement, although not expressly stated in the Constitution of the United States, remained as a fundamental underpinning of American democracy.

The importance of the freedom of mobility was firmly established in law, most forcefully in the twentieth century, in the case of *United States v. Wheeler*. The United States Supreme Court affirmed that every person "possessed the fundamental right, inherent in citizens of all free governments, peacefully to dwell within the limits of their respective States, to move at will from place to place therein, and to have free ingress thereto and egress therefrom, with a consequent authority in the States to forbid and punish violations of this fundamental right." The court confirmed mobility as central to a free society.

Slave owners in the American colonies restricted the physical mobility of their slaves but by custom and law also prevented social mobility. Although difficult, it might be possible for an indentured servant or a poor person to move up in social class. But for the enslaved, social mobility was impossible. They remained the property of their masters for life, and their children also faced lives as property. Wills and probate inventories listed the enslaved along with the pigs and the horses as chattel to be passed from generation to generation.

With the end of slavery, violence and threats enabled white community members to reinforce social control over Black communities in the South. The Klan, White Citizens' Councils and impromptu bands of vigilantes employed tactics that ranged from threatening their employment to

PLANTATION POLICE, OR HOME-GUARD, EXAMINING PASSES ON THE ROAD LEADING TO THE LEVEE OF THE MISSISSIPPI RIVER.
From a Sketch by F. B. Schell.

Slave patrols searched for enslaved people away from their plantations at night to check for runaways and to prevent enslaved people from gathering and possibly planning insurrections. *Frank B. Schell, "Plantation Police, Vicksburg, Miss.,"* Frank Leslie's Illustrated Newspaper, *July 11, 1863.*

intimidation and lynching to control the movement of African Americans. Restrictions on employment, housing and education kept Black people isolated in specific neighborhoods, restricting their mobility both physically and socially. In communities both small and large, white citizens required deference from Black people when they encountered them in public. They insisted that Black citizens step off the sidewalk or into doorways to let them pass. If two wagons came to a crossroads, the white person always had the right of way. In public accommodations—restaurants, hotels and movie theaters—Black people could be served only at the back door if at all or, in the case of movies, in the balcony. These practices reinforced the idea that African Americans were less than equal and could go only to those places where they were permitted.

The requirement that African Americans sit in the back of the bus was perhaps the most symbolic Jim Crow practice that reinforced restricted mobility. Jim Crow buses conveyed a resounding message that went beyond personal expressions of prejudice. With the segregation of buses, the state itself defined Black people as inferior and curtailed their movement. African American travelers also found segregated accommodations on trains and other public conveyances like streetcars and taxicabs. Often, passengers boarding a train above the Mason-Dixon line might be asked to move to a segregated train car to prevent the conductor from asking them to move once they crossed into the South. Even in the North, African Americans never knew how they might be greeted in a public space—with kindness or with disdain.

With the introduction of the automobile, African Americans found a mode of transportation that offered them personal freedom—the freedom to move about as they pleased. They loved their cars. Anyone who could purchase an automobile, new or used, did so. The automobile liberated Black drivers from the humiliation, fear and discomfort of riding on segregated buses and trains, as well as the danger of being physically assaulted. Cars also sheltered children from the taunts, racial epithets and stares that could accompany a ride on public conveyances. A private car provided an enclosed space that belonged to you. Shut off from the world, Black families rode in comfort and style. This newfound mobility opened up the nation to Black travelers as it had never been available before. Families who relocated to the North or West to live in cities like New York, Detroit, Newark, Pittsburgh, Philadelphia or Chicago as part of the Great Migration used their cars to return home to visit relatives. Their cars became symbols of their success, reflecting the move that many were making into the middle class, but also demonstrating their defiance of Jim Crow. Mobility served as a badge of honor. It said, *We will not be kept in "our place." We will not be second-class citizens*. With their disposable income, families visited vacation spots that welcomed Black tourists like Idlewild in Michigan, the Black beach at New Jersey's Atlantic City or Oak Bluffs on Martha's Vineyard, and they took their children to historic sites and monuments and to visit the nation's natural wonders like Niagara Falls.

One discriminatory practice actually facilitated the purchase of cars by Black families. Banks often colluded with realtors to prevent African Americans from purchasing houses and obtaining mortgages. When they could not purchase houses, usually a family's largest expense, Black families used their increasing discretionary income to buy cars, especially large heavy cars that made them feel safe and protected. A big car could also be practical if you had to sleep in it, since so many hotels practiced segregation, and a large trunk could be filled with coolers of food, blankets and pillows, suitcases, gallons of water and a large coffee can to use as a bathroom—everything you might need on the road and not be able to find.

Specialized businesses to support Black travelers sprang up across the country, particularly in urban centers. Guidebooks like the *Negro Motorist*

Americans loved their cars and often posed with them for family pictures. For African Americans, cars provided a special freedom that protected them from the humiliation of Jim Crow buses and segregated train cars. *Charles "Teenie" Harris Archive/Carnegie Museum of Art via Getty Images.*

Green Book, *Travelguide* and *The Go Guide* provided lists by state and city of the accommodations that welcomed them. In Pittsburgh, hotels for Black travelers dotted Wylie Avenue, and among the city's listings, one could also find tourist homes, service stations and beauty parlors. Dearing's Restaurant and Grill offered banquet spaces as well as "excellent cuisine" to locals and tourists alike. The menu included standard American fare, like porterhouse steaks and southern delicacies that appealed to new migrants. Baked southern corn pudding, green apple pie and fried chicken regularly appeared on the menu.[2]

The automobile dramatically changed the American landscape culturally and physically. For Americans today, it is difficult to imagine the world before cars, without gas stations, car dealerships, tire stores and myriad places to stop and eat or stay the night. Places like Pittsburgh's Scotty's Garage, a service unheard of before the automobile, became essential businesses in every town and city. Country lanes and dirt roads no wider than a single

Mechanics outside Scotty's Garage and Esso Station, 2414–16 Centre Avenue, Hill District, Pittsburgh, Pennsylvania, 1951. A variety of new businesses to support the automobile changed the American landscape. Black businesses flourished in a segregated world in which many white businesses would not serve Black travelers. *Charles "Teenie" Harris Archive/ Carnegie Museum of Art via Getty Images.*

wagon gave way to super multilane highways covered in macadam. Cars enabled families to move to the suburbs, expanding the footprint of urban areas. Air pollution accompanied the popularity of the automobile, and some people called it the devil wagon for that reason. But for African Americans, the mobility provided by the automobile was liberating and therapeutic in Jim Crow America.

Although the automobile became the preferred method of travel for African Americans, it was not a panacea for the racial roadblocks that Black travelers faced when they ventured out on the nation's roadways. Sometimes drivers found themselves stranded because of a mechanical problem with the car that no one would repair, or they could be stopped by law enforcement officers keen to enforce local segregationist attitudes. Tickets or steep fines were often the result of these encounters. Black drivers might stop at a restaurant or roadhouse that would not serve them, or worse, they could unknowingly drive into a hostile town with dire consequences. Some travelers encountered angry mobs of white citizens or police who shot or lynched the car's occupants. Segregation ended officially with the civil rights legislation signed by President Lyndon Johnson in 1964, but it would be another generation before many Black Americans felt that their mobility had truly expanded and that public accommodations were available to all Americans.

We have made progress since 1964. But there have also been setbacks. Ironically, while highways enabled African American travelers to avoid driving through unknown small towns, the building of highways, often a part of urban renewal, devastated many Black communities despite well-meaning intentions. In Pittsburgh, the Urban Redevelopment Authority, in its zeal to "protect" the city from flooding, pollution and "urban decay," displaced more than five thousand families. Public policy determined that businesses and homes in the city's Lower Hill District, the heart of the Black community, should be sacrificed and were torn down.[3] These redevelopment efforts resulted in the destruction of more than one thousand homes and many successful Black businesses. Displaced residents had few options except to move into public housing.[4]

In the twenty-first century, there remain challenges to Black mobility. Some communities in the United States still exclude African Americans as residents or are dangerous places for Black travelers. In 2017, the NAACP issued a travel advisory for the state of Missouri because of a variety of racist events within state borders. A national NAACP advisory that discouraged African Americans from visiting Missouri followed the state organization's recommendations. African Americans in Missouri are 75 percent more likely to be stopped by police than white residents, and the passage of a proposal in the Missouri legislature that would make it harder to sue for discrimination also contributed to the state's reputation.

Northern Black communities were not exempt from problems, particularly discrimination in housing and education, and Pittsburgh was no different. But the advantages of the automobile in the city provided increased physical mobility, as well as the opportunity for many families to move up into the middle class. "It is in Pittsburgh," wrote the *Pittsburgh Courier*, "that the great steel companies opened the 'Door of Opportunity' to the colored industrial worker."[5] Despite the difficulties faced by the community, the *Courier*'s writers saw Pittsburgh as a place where Black citizens could raise their children in "the midst of peace and plenty."

Chapter 2

BLACK MOBILITY

The Automobile's Role
in African American Autonomy

by Kimberly Cady, Associate Curator, Car and Carriage Museum,
the Frick Pittsburgh

Although the Reconstruction era immediately following the Civil War saw gains in political representation and equal citizenship for African Americans, the wins were short-lived. By the late 1880s, those gains were eliminated when elected white supremacist governments of the South, backed by terrorist organizations like the Ku Klux Klan, instituted so-called Jim Crow legislation to limit African Americans' access to the ballot. Jim Crow laws were a further extension of the Black Codes, proposed immediately following the war to restrict land and business ownership and the free movement of the newly emancipated. Jim Crow legislation ensured that the formerly enslaved knew that their place in society—second-class citizens—hadn't changed.

In addition to limiting full participation in their new citizenship by denying Blacks the right to vote, Jim Crow–era laws enforced segregation in schools, businesses and public transportation. The 1896 Supreme Court decision *Plessy v. Ferguson* codified segregation. This decision allowed companies and public entities to legally discriminate based on race so long as separate services (but not equal in a real sense) such as railcars, schools or water fountains were provided for Black citizens. *Plessy* remained in effect until 1954, when the Supreme Court ruled in favor of school integration in *Brown v. the Board of Education.*

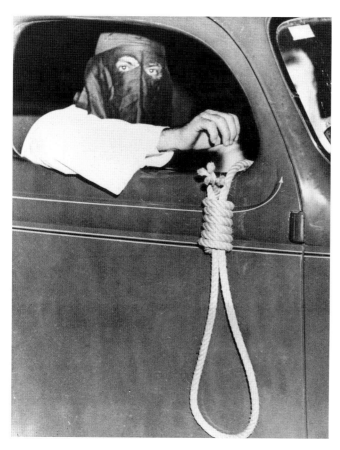

Top: A hangman's noose dangling from an automobile driven by a Ku Klux Klan member was a stark warning to Black voters to stay away from the polls during a 1939 election in Miami, Florida. Despite the threats, 616 Black people exercised their right to vote. *ID number 390503025, Associated Press*.

Bottom: Sharecroppers relied on sales of the year's harvest to pay their debts, with the selling price determined solely by the landowner. Since sharecroppers bought nearly all their supplies on credit—draft animals, land, seed and so on—they were often in debt to the landowner at the end of the season, essentially resulting in re-enslavement. *H. Armstrong Roberts/ClassicStock via Getty Images*.

Separate waiting rooms at train and bus stations, like this one in Durham, North Carolina, in 1940, were commonplace following the *Plessy v. Ferguson* ruling. *Library of Congress, Farm Security Administration—Office of War Information Photograph Collection.*

Until 1954, Black train passengers in the South had to sit not in the back but in the front: the first railcar behind the engine, where they endured the heat and soot produced by coal-burning locomotives. Streetcars offered "separate but equal" sections for Black and white passengers. Hailing a cab in the 1800s wasn't much different than today since hackney drivers could refuse to pick up a Black fare. Streetcar drivers could deny access to Black passengers or fabricate an offense to remove—and in some instances physically assault—these passengers. With the arrival of motorized public transportation in the 1930s, African Americans were relegated to the rear of buses over the hot engines and were required to give up their seats to white passengers. Refusal to abide by these laws could lead to harassment, arrest or even death.

Although white supremacist ideology and segregation existed across the nation, the restrictions on mobility, coupled with limited educational and economic resources in the South, led Blacks to migrate north as early as 1870 in search of better opportunities. Railroads were one of the first and largest industries to employ African Americans in the North in the late 1800s. Railroads recruited workers to fill positions from trackmen to porters.

Much like positions in manufacturing industries, there were almost no opportunities for advancement, although railroad work provided stability not found in sharecropping and agricultural work in the South. As World War I raged in Europe and paused European immigration to the United States, industries nationwide faced labor shortages. To combat the worker shortage, the Pennsylvania Railroad recruited southern Blacks in 1916 by offering free rides north. Like their early counterparts, however, the recruits were shut out of collective bargaining by the white-run labor unions, limiting once again their opportunity for advancement and higher wages. Some economic strides were made in 1925 when the Brotherhood of Sleeping Car Porters, organized by A. Philip Randolph, became the first African American union recognized by the American Federation of Labor.

A similar fate awaited African Americans in the steel industry. In the late 1800s, mills began recruiting African Americans as strikebreakers—derogatorily referred to as "scabs"—to end labor disputes. Regardless of skill level, the recruits were assigned the lowest-level, most dangerous,

Like buses, streetcars also subjected Black riders to segregated seating. Following Arkansas's passage of the Streetcar Segregation Act of 1903, Black leaders and members of the First Baptist Church of Little Rock organized a boycott and established a "we walk" league. *Birmingham, Alabama Public Library Archives.*

Although Black workers held the most dangerous positions—trackmen, brakemen or stoking the fire on a steam locomotive—working for the railroad, especially in the South, was a welcomed alternative to agricultural and domestic work. *Library of Congress, United States Military Railway Department.*

brutally harsh positions in the blast furnaces and rolling mills. "At the Jones and Laughlin facility in Pittsburgh, the entire boiler-room crew consisted of Black workers. Blacks predominated at the coke plant at the Clairton steelworks, and in most mills, they made up practically all of the labor gangs, especially in open-hearth and blast-furnace departments."[6]

In addition to the hazardous working conditions, manufacturing work for Blacks in the North was also boom or bust. Management sought to erode collective bargaining efforts by employing Black workers who were denied membership in the Amalgamated Association of Iron and Steelworkers. However, once management and the union reached an agreement, these workers often found themselves in unemployment lines hundreds of miles from home. During the wars, restricted European immigration and drafted laborers led to the remobilization of Black workers in manufacturing. Despite the unstable job market, dangerous working conditions and racial strife, by the start of World War II in Europe in the late 1930s, 1.6 million African Americans had made the journey out of the South.[7] For those who

The porter profession is credited with the development of the Black middle class. By the 1920s, the Pullman Company employed more than twenty thousand porters, making it the largest employer of Black workers in the United States. *Minnesota Historical Society via Getty Images.*

withstood the demanding labor conditions in the mills, the resulting wages enabled their transition into the middle class.

In the early twentieth century, African Americans who traveled to western Pennsylvania in search of the "promised land" found instead unstable and hazardous working conditions, segregated communities and overcrowded housing. By the end of World War II, however, they had made small advances in economic opportunity. By the 1940s, Black steelworkers accounted for more than 13 percent of the industry,[8] while Black women were hired at first as domestic labor and later by the manufacturing sector. Despite continued segregation in communities and professional fields, African Americans also became prominent teachers, ministers, doctors and businesspeople.

Although Black people in the region were beginning to prosper economically, they still faced an uphill battle when attempting to purchase affordable and livable housing. Practices like redlining (the unwritten racist policy of granting or denying home loans based on the

The Great Migration was one of the largest movements of people in United States history. From the 1910s through the 1960s, approximately six million Black citizens left the South for northern, midwestern and western states. *Library of Congress, Farm Security Administration—Office of War Information Photograph Collection.*

Pittsburgh's Hill District neighborhood was home to many Black-owned businesses, including the Powell Mercantile Company, seen here in 1935. *Courtesy of Archives and Special Collections, University of Pittsburgh Library System.*

Part of the New Deal's Works Progress Administration, the National Youth Association offered vocational training to young people ages sixteen to twenty-five. Typing was one of the skills offered through the Division of Negro Affairs in 1939. *Courtesy of Archives and Special Collections, University of Pittsburgh Library System.*

A Black-owned Hill District business, the Owl Cab Company, was founded in response to the Yellow Cab Company's refusal to pick up fares in the Black neighborhood. *Carnegie Museum of Art, Pittsburgh, Heinz Family Fund, Charles "Teenie" Harris Archive, 2001.35.34006.*

More than a means to get around, the car became a status symbol for Black Americans. The 1932 Chevy Confederate, known as the "Baby Cadillac," provided a means to display mobile wealth at a reasonable price. *Charles "Teenie" Harris Archive/Carnegie Museum of Art via Getty Images.*

applicant's geographic location) and housing covenants (contracts within deeds that prevented the sale of homes to African Americans in specific neighborhoods) hindered African Americans' path to attain the American dream. Since homeownership was out of reach for many African Americans, automobile ownership was one of the few paths to upward social mobility and challenging segregated spaces.

> *The twentieth century saw the rise of the automobile as the most important consumer product and economic lever in the United States. Driving became a required expression of American nationalism and citizenship. Yet American car culture was also inextricably intertwined with race. The automobile emerged as an important economic, technological, aesthetic, and racial category of North American identity and modernity in the twentieth century.*[9]

By 1916, automobiles had transitioned from a plaything of the very wealthy to a necessary tool. Henry Ford's standardization of assembly-line production lowered car prices and made car ownership attainable for many.

Left: In 1939, the Ford Tudor was a moderately priced sedan (Standard $680 or De Luxe $745) with styling mimicking the more expensive Lincoln Zephyr. Although it was one of the more affordable cars on the market, it did not offer much in the way of technical or safety advances. *Courtesy Elizabeth A. Burns & J. Lawrence Burns Collection.*

Below: The average assembly-line worker could purchase a Ford Model T with four months' pay in 1914. *Courtesy the Frick Pittsburgh, 1999.1.9. Gift of the estate of G. Whitney Snyder.*

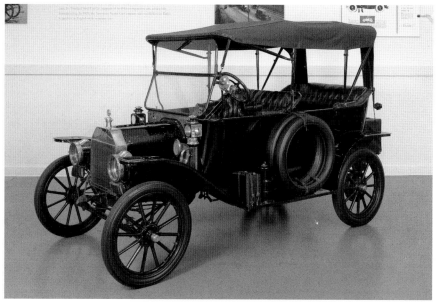

Likewise, Ford's $5 day for assembly workers made it possible for them to purchase the automobiles they produced.[10] By 1923, a new Ford Model T could be had for as little as $265—15 percent of a well-paid Pullman Porter's annual salary of $1,800.[11] Access to an automobile meant freedom to travel wherever and whenever one liked, without the restraints of public transportation routes and schedules.

For Black motorists, a car also reduced their experience of overt discrimination and violence. Public transportation—buses, streetcars and trains—were the domain of whites. As operators and passengers, they enforced segregation and how Black riders could move within those spaces: whether a Black passenger could sit or stand, arrive at their desired destination or be removed from the conveyance for a fabricated offense. The operator's decision was backed by law enforcement, leaving Black passengers with few options for legal reprisal. For African Americans, car ownership was a mobile symbol of "making it" while also providing increased privacy and safety.

Those who could afford a new car still faced discrimination when purchasing at a dealership. Black salespeople were nonexistent at first, and once hired, they were not permitted on the showroom floor but rather relegated to an out-of-sight office. White salespeople were not accommodating to Black customers, and some manufacturers, such as Cadillac, at first refused to sell to Black motorists. Although Black celebrities and athletes favored Cadillacs, the company once had an unwritten yet understood policy that dealerships would not sell to Black consumers. To acquire a Cadillac, Black buyers would pay as much as $300 for a white proxy to purchase the car.[12] It wasn't until 1940 that the first Black-owned new car dealership was established when Ed Davis, a salesman for Chrysler in Detroit, was offered a Studebaker franchise to increase the company's Black sales market in the region.[13] Since they were often denied loans for new cars, Black buyers relied on the used car market.

Most Black shoppers chose cars based less on style and status and more on safety and reliability. When selecting a car, Black consumers tended to trust companies that advertised reliability and safety, like Dodge's slogan, "Reliable, Dependable, Sound," or Buick's, "When better automobiles are built, Buick will build them." The most affordable were Fords and Chevys, but luxury makes like Buick, Cadillac and Lincoln were among the most popular for size, dependability and innovation.

Size was especially important. Because of continued segregation and discrimination at roadside businesses—service stations, restaurants and

Although car ownership lessened the chance for racial discrimination, it did not eliminate it. Black motorists traveled with supplies—extra gas, spare parts and tools— long after service stations became commonplace. *Library of Congress, Farm Security Administration—Office of War Information Photograph Collection.*

With a car, Black families were able to set their own course for travel, unrestricted by bus lines and trains. *Courtesy Elizabeth A. Burns & J. Lawrence Burns Collection.*

Founded in 1902 from the remains of the failed Henry Ford Company (precursor to Ford Motor Company), Cadillac quickly emerged as a premier luxury American brand due to the engineering prowess of its founder, Henry Leland. *Courtesy Elizabeth A. Burns & J. Lawrence Burns Collection.*

In an effort to increase slumping sales during the Depression, Nicholas Dreystadt, head of Cadillac's Service Division, recommended eliminating Cadillac's discriminatory sales policy and opening the sales market to Black consumers. *Courtesy of the Western Reserve Historical Society, Cleveland, Ohio.*

Above: Racial tensions at the Chrysler dealership where Ed Davis worked as a salesman led him to venture out independently. Studebaker offered Davis a franchise in 1940, a year after successfully establishing his used car business. *From the Collection of the Studebaker National Museum, South Bend, Indiana.*

Left: Ed Davis was the first African American awarded a Big Three franchise. He retired from his Chrysler-Plymouth dealership in 1971. *Walter P. Reuther Library, Wayne State University.*

Top: Theodore MacManus, a copywriter for Dodge, coined the word "dependability." Dodge began using the term in advertising materials around 1914. *Courtesy Elizabeth A. Burns & J. Lawrence Burns Collection.*

Bottom: Buicks were some of the most popular models among Black consumers. They were chosen not only for size and comfort but also for their quick acceleration, a potentially lifesaving feature for Black motorists. *Courtesy Elizabeth A. Burns & J. Lawrence Burns Collection.*

Top: The Buick Series 60 was the companion to the larger top-priced Roadmaster, featuring the same powerful engine at a more affordable price. Named for the famous 20th Century Limited passenger train, it provided quiet, quick and comfortable travel in the grandest style, much like its namesake. *Courtesy The NB Center for American Automotive Heritage.*

Middle: Introduced by Ford for the 1939 production year, the medium-priced Mercury 8 fit neatly between the basic Ford and the upscale Lincoln. Long and unusually wide, the Mercury offered vast room for passengers and luggage. *From the Collections of The Henry Ford.*

Bottom: Chevy introduced a lightweight truck series in 1947. An ideal vehicle for farmers, a profession still dominated by African Americans, the new design featured higher seats and larger windows for better visibility and a hauling capacity of up to a ton. *Courtesy of the Western Reserve Historical Society, Cleveland, Ohio.*

hotels—Black buyers needed an automobile with enough storage space to transport extra supplies. Gas, spare tires and tools were useful for impromptu repairs when denied roadside service. Another critical feature was a comfortable and spacious interior for the long-distance drives that might end with sleeping in the car if the travelers were refused lodging at a motel. Likewise, cars with the latest innovations like power steering and automatic transmissions were easier to operate and reduced the chance of unwanted encounters with other drivers or law enforcement if the car broke down. As African Americans became more mobile—traveling for work and leisure—selecting a dependable vehicle was only the first step. They also had to navigate the safest route to travel before even getting behind the wheel.

Private car ownership was not without its dangers. Black drivers planning a long trip often chose to begin their journey at night. Night driving made it harder to determine the driver's skin color, alleviating some of the dangers of being harassed by white drivers or police on the highway. Traveling on country roads at night could be particularly unsafe, and finding accommodations—especially south of the Mason-Dixon line or west of Chicago—could be challenging. Drivers often chose to continue through the night, fighting sleep and fatigue, to reach their destination by early morning or midday.[14] Black motorists also had to think about everyday travel behind the wheel, a concern that continues today. It was not unheard of to be pulled over by law enforcement for the infraction of being a Black driver. Officers would question the legitimacy of the owner, asking, "Who owns this car?" or, "How could you afford this car?" To avoid this line of questioning, but no less humiliating, a Black driver might keep a chauffeur's cap in the car and, when asked about ownership, respond that he was a driver taking his employer's maid and children home. The threat of violence was so prevalent that this trope—Black driver as chauffeur—was used when Blacks and whites traveled in cars together, most notably during the Freedom Rides of the 1960s.

It wasn't just in the South that Black drivers had to be wary. Racism was prevalent across the United States. Without warning, drivers could find themselves in a "sundown town."[15] These were white-only towns dotting the map from Massachusetts to California that prohibited African Americans from living there or staying after sunset. Police-backed violence and intimidation ensured that Black motorists were across town or county lines before dark. Travelers would often come upon a sundown town unexpectedly, encountering an unwelcoming sign at the township line or on a banner flying above Main Street. Such risks to Black drivers were

Black drivers encountered various discriminatory signs along the highways, including this one that was meant to intimidate residents at a housing project in Michigan in 1942. *Library of Congress, Farm Security Administration—Office of War Information Photograph Collection.*

"A shocking example of bad taste," claimed a Pittsburgh judge who reluctantly had to honor a contract between the Pittsburgh Outdoor Advertising Company and the Republican Party in 1949. The fearmongering ad was produced for the 1949 Pittsburgh mayoral campaign. *Charles "Teenie" Harris Archive/Carnegie Museum of Art via Getty Images.*

genuine and required extensive planning before even getting behind the wheel. Many would rely on the experiences of friends or family when planning routes and stops.

However, by the 1930s, Black travelers didn't have to navigate these treacherous roadways alone. While widely read Black newspapers like the *Pittsburgh Courier* and the *Chicago Defender* helped bring southern migrants north, once they arrived, printed travel guides—marketed directly to African Americans—helped them know where it was safe to eat, sleep and gas up.[16] Equally important, they let travelers know where not to go. Mainstream travel brochures, like those produced by the American Automobile Association at the time, focused on white-owned businesses, many of which were not accessible to Black motorists. Those that did serve Black patrons might have "special rules," such as "colored" entrances or sections, which were only discovered by the motorist after making a societal misstep that could result in humiliation or harassment.

Beginning in 1930 with *Hackley and Harrison's Hotel and Apartment Guide* and later *Grayson's Travel and Business Guide* (1937) and Victor Green's *The Negro Motorist Green Book* (1937), Black vacationers could plan the safest route for their journey. These guides advertised Black-owned and white-owned but Black-friendly businesses where travelers could find a meal or a night's rest without the threat of harm. The *Green Book*, as it was called, ceased production in 1967, three years after the passage of the Civil Rights Act, which officially banned racial discrimination in public places and aimed to end Jim Crow laws. At that time, the Black-owned businesses that once thrived in segregated communities began to decline as Black tourists had more choices.

The automobile brought a modicum of freedom and autonomy to the Black community, and in 1955, it also aided in the fight to end segregation on public transportation in the South. Claudette Colvin was arrested on a bus in Montgomery, Alabama, when she refused to give up her seat and move to the rear. Later that year, Rosa Parks was arrested for the same offense. Following these arrests, the Women's Political Council (WPC) called for a boycott of the Montgomery City Bus Lines to combat Jim Crow segregation.[17] The WPC purchased cars and organized a carpool service to ensure that Black workers could still get to work while boycotting the bus. The boycott's success was driven by access to and mobilizing around the automobile.

Although car ownership and the automobile in general brought opportunities and benefits to the Black community, its effects were not all

Top: Between 1939 and 1967, fifteen Black-owned or Black-friendly hotels and six tourist homes were listed in the *Green Book*. The Palace Hotel at 1549 Wylie Avenue in the Hill District first appeared in 1947. *Carnegie Museum of Art, Pittsburgh, Charles "Teenie" Harris Archive, 2001.35.11340.*

Bottom: Travelers could also find information about services such as gas stations and car repair in the *Green Book*. Even celebrities like crooner Nat "King" Cole, seen here with his wife, Maria, might have used the *Green Book* to find the Owl Cab Company, one of the only car services that traveled to the Hill. *Charles "Teenie" Harris Archive/ Carnegie Museum of Art via Getty Images.*

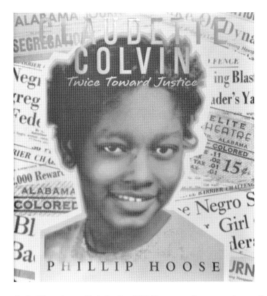 

Left: Claudette Colvin (b. 1939), an active member of the NAACP Youth Council, was only fifteen years old when she was convicted on two counts of violating Montgomery's segregation laws and one count of assaulting an officer. *Gordon Chibroski/*Portland Press Herald *via Getty Images.*

Right: The arrest of Rosa Parks (1913–2005) nine months after Colvin's arrest brought needed attention to segregation. She was an accomplished activist who had worked with the NAACP on other civil rights issues. *Library of Congress, Prints and Photographs Division.*

Station wagons like the Chevy Nomad were added to the boycott's carpool fleet by the WPC because they could hold more passengers. *Courtesy the General Motors Heritage Center.*

positive. The postwar boom of the 1950s brought about urban sprawl, the suburbs, highway expansion and urban renewal. Suburbs and urban sprawl developed as white homeowners fled their newly diverse neighborhoods and cities, a phenomenon known as White Flight. The highway expansion program, created to accommodate this movement, deliberately decimated Black communities—demolishing homes and businesses to create highways that divided neighborhoods. Many of the targeted communities had grown and thrived during segregation, their businesses serving Black patrons when others would not. In addition to the loss of homes and businesses, the new highways brought congestion, noise, air pollution and illness to the residents who remained. Pittsburgh was not immune to urban renewal. Evidence of it exists today with the expansion of Interstate 79 and the construction of the Civic Arena in the lower Hill District.[18]

Although the successes of the civil rights movement ended segregated public accommodations, racial profiling for "driving while Black" continues to torment Black motorists. Black and Brown drivers still have a higher

Considered a "blight" in the 1950s, the Bethel AME Church, founded in 1808, was seized through eminent domain by the Urban Redevelopment Authority of Pittsburgh and demolished in 1957. *Charles "Teenie" Harris Archive/Carnegie Museum of Art via Getty Images.*

Left: Once a leading jazz club on the East Coast touring circuit, the Crawford Grill No. 1 met the same fate as the Bethel AME Church—demolished in 1956 to make way for the Civic Arena. *Charles "Teenie" Harris Archive/ Carnegie Museum of Art via Getty Images.*

Below: When the Civic Arena opened in 1961, 1,300 buildings had been razed, displacing eight thousand residents and closing four hundred businesses in the Lower Hill, one of Pittsburgh's oldest neighborhoods. *Charles "Teenie" Harris Archive/ Carnegie Museum of Art via Getty Images.*

In response to the destruction of the Lower Hill, the Citizens Committee for Hill District Renewal and the Pittsburgh branch of the NAACP erected a billboard in 1961 calling for a halt to redevelopment and urging the construction of affordable housing, a call that still echoes today. *Charles "Teenie" Harris Archive/Carnegie Museum of Art via Getty Images.*

rate of being pulled over for minor driving infractions and risk uncertainty with every traffic stop.[19] African American car buyers in the mid-twentieth century faced higher insurance premiums and more difficulty in car loan approvals due to discriminatory policies employed by dealers and banks. Despite a growing Black consumer market, automobile manufacturers would not directly market to Black consumers until the 1970s, when they began advertising in *Ebony* and *Jet* magazines. Even with its challenges, African Americans, perhaps more than any other demographic of drivers, recognized the literal and figurative mobility the car could provide. The Great Migration moved six million African Americans from the southern region of the United States to parts north and west, and the automobile provided further freedom of movement once they arrived.

Chapter 3

THE *PITTSBURGH COURIER* DURING THE GREAT MIGRATION, 1910–50

by Samuel W. Black, Director, African American Program, Senator John Heinz History Center

The *Pittsburgh Courier* began about 1908 as a small pamphlet-type sheet hand-delivered to readers. Its creator had no way of knowing how important the *Courier* would become or its impact on migrating African Americans. But by the 1950s, it would be one of the more significant vehicles used by migrants to acclimate themselves to life in Pittsburgh. The Great Migration to Pittsburgh can be charted by two phases: the first from 1900 to 1930 and the second from 1940 to 1960. Each phase increased the African American population in the city, and each had its own characteristic migrants. These were not only the formative years of what came to be known as the Great Migration but also the formative years of the *Pittsburgh Courier*. The *Courier* itself was started by a migrant, Edwin Nathaniel Harleston. Harleston migrated to Pittsburgh from Charleston, South Carolina, by way of Atlantic City, New Jersey. He brought his writing skills to Pittsburgh in search of a readership and to find a place in a growing migrant community. His 1907 book, *The Toiler's Life*, was his first known venture into the literary world.[20] Harleston was originally from Charleston and quite possibly named his African American paper after the *Charleston Courier*.[21] He had few connections when he arrived in the smoky city in 1907, but the connections he did have were significant ones.

Before migrating to Pittsburgh, Harleston lived a few blocks from Parthenia Tanner, an Atlantic City teacher from a well-known Pittsburgh family. It was Tanner who became the connection to Pittsburgh for Harleston. After moving to Pittsburgh, he took a room in the Tanner home on Winthrop Avenue in Oakland.[22] Harleston, looking for investors in his newspaper idea, soon approached the family of his landlord. As a result, the Tanner family put him in touch with members of the Loendi Club, an African American men's professional organization that gathered investors for the paper. Support came from club members Hepburn Carter, Edward Penman, William Nelson Page, William Hance, Samuel Rosemond and Cumberland Posey Sr. The group then engaged a recent graduate of the University of Pittsburgh School of Law, Robert L. Vann, to incorporate the company as the Pittsburgh Courier Publishing Company in 1910. The first issue of the paper was published in January with Posey as its first president, Harleston as editor, Reverend Scott Wood as city editor, Carter as advertising manager and Marion Tanner as subscription manager.[23]

Edwin Nathaniel Harleston, about 1907. Frontispiece of *The Toiler's Life* (Philadelphia: Jensen Press, 1907).

Robert L. Vann arrived in Pittsburgh as a student from North Carolina. He attended Virginia Union University before enrolling at Western Pennsylvania University (now University of Pittsburgh) on a Charles Avery Scholarship, graduating in 1906. He then enrolled in law school, where he became its first African American graduate in 1909.[24] Within the *Courier*'s first year of publication, Vann assumed a leadership role, joining

Robert L. Vann, about 1909. *Courtesy of Archives and Special Collections, University of Pittsburgh Library System.*

Harleston as co-editor. The paper's office was in Vann's law office on Wiley Avenue but was printed in Atlantic City under Harleston's watch. Within a year, Harleston had moved to New York City, and Vann became sole editor of the paper. The leadership of the paper was composed of migrants to Pittsburgh from southern states: Posey, Wood, Harleston, Vann and business manager Ira Lewis (added in 1914). They knew the plight of the migrant and understood the challenges and opportunities possible in Pittsburgh.

When the *Courier* began publication in January 1910, Pittsburgh's African American population was 24,623—4.8 percent of the city's population of 533,905. In ten years, the 1920 African American population had increased to 37,725. The city population had nominal growth because of the decrease in European immigration caused by World War I, with growth of just 10.2 percent, to 588,343.[25] The *Courier*'s leadership wanted to capitalize on the migrant growth and recognized that the paper had a responsibility to speak to the profile of migration. Within two years, its masthead listed 10,000 weekly readers. The prevailing thought is that African Americans migrated from the South to northern cities looking for jobs, family, opportunity and to escape Jim Crow and oppression. What they found in Pittsburgh and elsewhere was marginalization, segregation and struggle. Those migrants who came for education or already had education found a different avenue of opportunity in a growing middle class. Vann, a student migrant, found success in his law practice within years of receiving his degree. But the unskilled and uneducated migrants found difficulty moving up the ladder of success and fulfilling the promise that northern cities were supposed to offer.

Migrants willed the opportunities not bestowed on them to their children who migrated with them or were born in Pittsburgh. From 1910 to 1920, 60 percent of migrants came from the states of Alabama, Georgia, North Carolina and Virginia. Unlike the migration of the nineteenth century that was heavily from Virginia, this twentieth-century migration was primarily from Alabama.[26] Once in Pittsburgh, the migrants found the need to adjust to the social and economic climate of the city. Socially, "OPs" (Old Pittsburghers) treated poor migrants with contempt. OPs were Pittsburghers "proud of having been in the city before the Great Migration."[27] Over time, these biases subsided as migrants became part of the fabric of Black Pittsburgh. This early period of the migration brought not only Vann and Harleston to town but also jazz music greats like Mary Lou Williams (Georgia), Billy Strayhorn (Ohio) and Negro League baseball great Josh Gibson (Georgia).

Between 1910 and 1930, the Great Migration more than doubled the population of African Americans in Allegheny County, from 34,217 to 83,326.[28] Within this wave were seasonal laborers—those who returned to southern farms during harvest or planting season. When they returned south, they took the *Pittsburgh Courier* with them.[29] This phenomenon helped to expand the *Courier*'s readership and provided valuable information about

Left: Portrait of Mary Lou Williams, New York, circa 1946. *William P. Gottlieb/Ira and Leonore S. Gershwin Fund Collection, Music Division, Library of Congress.*

Right: Josh Gibson with the Pittsburgh Crawfords, where he played from 1932 to 1936. *Courtesy the National Baseball Hall of Fame and Museum.*

life in Pittsburgh. But all was not so pleasant for African American migrants during its earlier stages. The newspaper reported on the squalid conditions in which many migrants lived. A 1912 report noted that African Americans owned 681 properties worth $2.5 million.[30] The numbers might have looked impressive in 1912, but 681 property owners out of 35,000-plus residents indicates a large class of renters. Some of the landlords were among those 681 property owners. The rise in migration increased the desperate living conditions in the Hill District, Northside and other communities. But unlike many of their parents, who migrated from southern states that did not provide schools or had segregated and below-standard schools, students had greater opportunities for a kindergarten through twelfth-grade education in Pittsburgh. The city opened several new high schools to deal with the increase in student populations. From 1911 to 1930, new high schools opened in the city: Peabody (1911), South Hills (1913), Schenley (1916), Westinghouse (1917), Perry (1923), Oliver (1925), Taylor Allderdice (1927), Carrick (1929) and Connelly Vocational (1930). These high schools fed the growing population in Pittsburgh as European immigrants and African American migrants moved into the city. The migration changed the demographics of

A segregated waiting room at Union Terminal train station in Jacksonville, Florida, 1920s. *State Library and Archives of Florida.*

several Pittsburgh neighborhoods. During this period, the multiethnic Hill District became majority African American. The Lower Hill District became a magnet for European immigrants and African American migrants. But the war in Europe cut off the flow of immigrants, especially from eastern Europe. From 1915 through the 1920s, the Hill District gained some 14,000 African American residents and lost 7,600 Europeans.[31]

The Hill District is central in any discussion of African American history and migration to the city. The *Courier* office was in the community, as was Vann's law office. The paper's reporters had a front-row seat on all the demographic changes that socially and politically impacted the growth of the community. The paper included listings of borough and township community news that often reported on family and social gatherings. One can gauge the travel culture from these notices. Most accommodations discriminated against Black travelers, so private homes often accepted friends and acquaintances. Newspaper columns included "Afro-American Cullings," "Local News" and "Secret Society Notices," which reported on travels of Pittsburghers and visitors to the city. In addition, news and correspondence from reginal boroughs and communities such as Altoona,

Housing conditions, circa 1920–30. *Courtesy of Archives and Special Collections, University of Pittsburgh Library System.*

Washington, Sewickley and New Castle attracted the attention of longtime residents and migrants to those communities.

The paper's distribution followed the railroad lines. Pittsburgh was a major hub with connections in each direction and each of these communities. For instance, in Sewickley, the railroad provided jobs such as porters, cooks and servers on the trains and helped build the community's middle-class profile. Social and cultural associations made the migration experience bearable and helped with settlement, employment and connections to new social circles. Men and women associated with Odd Fellows, Prince Hall Masons, Elk and other fraternal groups made connections through their lodges. One of the most important institutions that aided in the migration and settlement of migrants was the African American church. The paper regularly reported on activities of these groups, making them a significant part of community life.

Journalist and scholar Ervin Dyer talked about migration experiences and motives for moving out of the South when he interviewed migrants for a *Pittsburgh Post-Gazette* article. Eighty-four-year-old Homewood resident David Blakely recalled his reasons for moving out of the South: "I dunno anything about a Great Migration. All I know is I left because I was tired of not being able to vote and not being treated like a citizen." Dyer documents Blakely's 1947 journey from Florida to New York City and then to Pittsburgh.[32] Blakely found the opportunity to vote in Pittsburgh absent of Jim Crow restriction; he even found African American candidates to vote for. A *Courier* editorial in November 1948 mentioned the killing of two Georgia men trying to vote in that state.[33] As usual, the *Courier* was making a point about the differences in living in the South and the North. These differences extended to political affiliations as well. There were countermeasures taken by white power structure in the South to maintain its African American population as a cheap labor force. In an article titled "The Way to Stop Migration," the paper talked about the efforts of southerners to do "everything in [their] power and out to keep the Negro there." Negroes were being lied to about "long freezing winters, smallpox epidemics, the high cost of living, lack of sympathy and understanding on the part of Northern whites."[34]

Fifteen years before David Blakely migrated to Pittsburgh, the big question was which political party the growing African American community would align with. Robert L. Vann forecasted the shift from the Republican to the Democratic Party in 1932. He was leaning toward Democratic presidential candidate Franklin D. Roosevelt and his plan to address the Depression conditions on the economy. Vann monitored the impact of both parties and their failure to follow through on campaign promises. Vann publicly announced his decision in a speech on September 11, 1932, in Cleveland, Ohio, at the St. James African Methodist Episcopal Church Forum. In suggesting that African Americans, who were majority Republican at the time, change their political allegiance to Roosevelt's Democrats, Vann said, "My friends, go turn the picture of Abraham Lincoln to the wall." The *Courier* headline read, "GOP Is Flayed by Vann" in a front-page article on September 17, 1932.[35]

Another reason for migration to Pittsburgh was the opportunity for jobs in the steel mills and peripheral industries. The truth is, most of the major mills in 1915 hired only a small percentage of African American workers. By 1916, Carnegie Steel was the largest employer of African American millworkers, employing 4,000 men. Jones & Laughlin employed 1,500; Westinghouse Electric 900.[36] Many were kept out of jobs by discrimination in labor unions. Editor Vann urged African Americans to form their own labor unions to counteract race discrimination by largely white unions.[37] The threat white unions held against the mills was taken seriously, and Vann knew it. Very few African Americans who were hired by the mills obtained high-

Henton Herron, a 1910 migrant from Alabama who worked in the Vandergrift Steel Works, on the porch of his home with family members Lois Miles and Sally Millage. *Senator John Heinz History Center, Gift of Lois Miles.*

level jobs. Joe W. Trotter, historian of migration and the urban experience, notes that John Harley and William Dennon, graduates of the University of Pittsburgh, worked as a draftsman and engineer, respectively. *Courier* trustee William Nelson Page served as a private secretary to W.G. Gayle, general manager of sales for Carnegie Steel.[38] These professional positions in the mills were exceptions because most African American millworkers were denied promotions and assigned to the low-level jobs that were also the most hazardous. Among the immediate economic causes of the migration were the labor depression in the South in 1914 and 1915 and the large decrease in foreign immigration resulting from the world war. Then came the cotton boll weevil in the summers of 1915 and 1916, greatly damaging the cotton crop over a considerable area, largely in Louisiana, Mississippi, Alabama, Georgia and Florida, and unsettled farming conditions in 1917.[39]

But migrants from the South were also escaping racial oppression under Jim Crow customs—legal and de facto. Every aspect of life was impacted by oppression. African Americans were eager to leave these conditions and did so by various means, be it train, automobile or some form of public transportation. Only later did air travel become viable for migrants, but rarely. From the 1910s into the '30s and '40s, the population of communities like the Hill District became increasingly Black. The population of African Americans in 1950 stood around 82,500.[40] By this time, the *Courier* had become the most circulated African American weekly paper in the country. Child migrants and the children of migrants became *Courier* newspaper boys. Activist and elected official Sala Udin was a newsboy when he lived in the Lower Hill. He delighted in the cadence of the newsboy call, "*Pittsburgh Courier!*"

African American migrants to Pittsburgh between 1910 and 1950 changed the city and the experiences of African Americans alike. The *Pittsburgh Courier* newspaper served as a guide and communication post for migrants and those looking to change their conditions. As much as the Great Migration changed America, it also made Pittsburgh a world-class city as the influx of Black life and culture increasingly challenged existing biases and discrimination. The *Courier* made it a campaign to provide news and opinions on the condition of Black life. Its reporting on the migration often connected the Pittsburgh phenomenon with national trends in Chicago, Philadelphia or other northern cities. Subtly, in the pages of the paper there was often a mention of a "Mr. So and So" visiting relatives or friends in some Borough or Hill District home. "Mr. So and So," a migrant, relied on the *Courier* not only as his introduction to Pittsburgh but also his introduction to a life without most southern Jim Crow conditions. So, this newspaper—started by migrants and aiding other migrants—became the largest-circulated African American weekly of its time and helped make Pittsburgh a great American city.

Chapter 4

THE GREAT MIGRATION AND AFRICAN AMERICAN STEELWORKERS

by Ron Baraff, Director of Historic Resources and Facilities, Rivers of Steel

*These are some of the things that we want to know about Pittsburgh. We are
familiar with its smoke and factories, its politics and religion; its crime and
justice; its housing program for blacks and whites. We know of its wealth and
how little of it the Negro is permitted to own temporarily. But what we don't
know is how the Mayor of the City or the Chamber of Commerce can plead to
disregard creed and color, to aid in disseminating information about Pittsburgh,
when the facts plainly show that in the schedule of things we have been considered
as nonentities. We want to "Know Pittsburgh"—but we want Pittsburgh to
know us—without creed or color.*[41]
—*John L. Clark,* Pittsburgh Courier, *February 20, 1926*

As we push forward further into the deindustrialized age, the lessons
of the Pittsburgh region's industrial past are not to be forgotten.
Between 1880 and 1921, the floodgates opened to receive a torrent
of southern and eastern European immigrants into America. While there
were many pull factors for their emigration from their homelands, most
immigrants who came into the region were drawn by the prospect of jobs
within the burgeoning iron, steel, coke and coal industries. These southern
and eastern European immigrants who flocked by the thousands to western
Pennsylvania left an indelible mark on the industry and the region. Vestiges
of their ethnicity, culture and lineage are still recognizable today. That

said, while their stories are deservedly celebrated and remembered, there is another group of immigrants who came into this region who are often overlooked, ignored and underappreciated.

Known as the Great Migration,[42] this first major exodus of African Americans from the American South to the northern, midwestern and western states during the era of 1910–40 is one of the largest movements of people in our nation's history. They were pushed out of the Jim Crow South by increasing racial violence, segregation, oppression and crop failures due to floods, the destructive boll weevil and low crop prices, as well as lack of educational and economic opportunities. The first great wave of migration came during World War I as northern workers were sent off to the armed forces, creating a void in the labor force and new opportunities for men from the South to work in the manufacturing industries of the North. African Americans made up a substantial portion of the unskilled workers in the iron and steel industries by the middle of the twentieth century. While providing hope for their future, most of the newcomers found it hard to advance in the mills and discovered that discrimination in the industrialized North was not all that different than it was in the South. In some cases, it was even worse. They found themselves stuck in the worst, lower-paying jobs, in the worst of working conditions.

"During the war," said Bishop Clair, "Negros [*sic*] were invited to come North and take the place of laborers who were serving in the army, and in the North, they found better wages, schools and social conditions. At the end of the war," he said, "the Negro did not want to go back South. His letters to friends in the South caused more Negros to go North."[43]

As with the wartime shortage of labor, the postwar growth of the iron and steel industries gave rise to employment opportunities for African Americans. Black laborers were openly recruited from southern communities to come north. These recruiters, both white and Black men, were sent to the South by northern manufacturing companies. They were often derogatorily referred to as "jacklegs,"[44] a term that by its very definition connotes a sense of dishonesty or unscrupulousness. Jacklegs were most often charismatic and educated men, self-styled religious leaders who were often in a position of power and trust, a minister or preacher. In *Blood on the Forge*, William Attaway's seminal novel on the Great Migration published in 1941, the protagonists of the story, the Moss brothers, are repeatedly warned to stay away from the jackleg recruiters, but they succumb to one anyway. The recruiter's mantra: good men like them are needed up north—plenty of them—to work in the mills where they would find success and a future that they are lacking in the

South. The Moss brothers agree to a midnight rendezvous at Masonville Junction, where the jackleg has arranged for them to hop on a boxcar for the ride north to the mills of western Pennsylvania.

> *The Moss brothers, crammed in with other black workers, are herded by sealed train to Vaughn, a mill town of rain, slag, soot, garbage, dirt roads, and prostitutes stinking under their perfume. The banks of the Monongahela are lined with red ore, yellow limestone, and black coke, a stark contrast to the landscape they grew up in that Big Mat, especially, never fails to note.*[45]

Of course, not all recruiters or jacklegs were nefarious. One such real-life jackleg is recalled by his son Herb Edwards, who was a longtime western Pennsylvania artist and former steelworker. Herb's family came to the region from Tennessee. Of the seven children in the family, Herb was the only one born in the North. His family was drawn there "because of economics." Herb's father was a rarity because he was educated—a college graduate. "Now, we're talking turn-of-the-century," Herb said in an interview. Because he was a good public speaker, Herb's father, who was living in Allenport, Pennsylvania, and working for the Pittsburgh Steel Company at the time, was asked to become a recruiter—a jackleg. The mill would send him south, where he would recruit men to come north to work for Pittsburgh Steel. The men would be given transportation and a promise of a job to leave behind all that they had known for the prospects of a better life and work. For his efforts, he would receive a bonus and all his expenses would be paid if he were successful in his endeavors. His interactions with the recruited men did not end there: Herb's father, still in the employ and under the guise of Pittsburgh Steel, would teach night classes for the people he brought up from the South. Akin to the Americanization classes sponsored by the industry for newly arrived southern and eastern Europeans, he was charged with teaching the men the basics—how to read and sign their names.[46]

Another pull factor for the industrial North was the labor issues confronting the industry in the late nineteenth and early twentieth centuries. African American workers were first used as strikebreakers in the Pittsburgh region during the Homestead Strike of 1892, often recruited from southern iron mills, bringing with them a much-needed skill set. While the number of strikebreakers in 1892 was not high, it did set a precedent for future labor issues. Chief among these was the Great Steel Strike of 1919, commonly known as the Hunky Strike.

African American Class Carnegie Steel, circa 1920. *Courtesy of Rivers of Steel, Bilcsik Collection.*

Such was the case for John Hughey's family. John was employed at United States Steel's Carrie Blast Furnaces in Rankin and Swissvale, Pennsylvania, from 1947 through 1982, when the mill ceased production. John was born in 1925 in Rankin, Pennsylvania, a community abutting the Carrie complex. John's father had moved to Pittsburgh in 1919, coming from South Carolina. He had been recruited by a man—a jackleg like Herb Edward's father— who spoke of better jobs and opportunities up north and the possibilities that would come with working in the booming steel industry in Pittsburgh. Seeking that hope of a better life, John's father had moved to the Pittsburgh area, where he was employed in the Edgar Thomson Works in Braddock, as he described in an interview:

> **John Hughey***: My dad worked in the Edgar Thomson mill. He was born in Jenkinsville, South Carolina. And he came up in here in 1919 and was hired into the Edgar Thomson work when they had the great strike of 1919. And I had one, two, three, four brothers that worked in the mill for a short period of time....I said, my father was brought up here in 1919, but because he was brought up here to break a strike. Because at that time they were trying to organize. SWOC* [Steel Workers Organizing

Committee] *was trying to organize the mills and organize them to break their strikes back in that day…but bring the minorities up to break the strike, give them good jobs…and as soon as the strike was over, they would throw them out on the street, and they become gardeners and wherever they can handle. And then that's why they were up here as second-class citizens.*

Q*: When your dad came up in the 1919 strike, did he realize, I mean, did they tell him upfront that he was coming up to help break a strike? Or did they just tell him that there were good jobs up there?*

John Hughey*: Yeah, they just told them there were good jobs. Back then they didn't know…coming out of the South. My dad coming out—born in South Carolina…he came up and he didn't know what he was going to… was told he have a better job. Then as he got out, he didn't have a job after the strike was over. So, they transported him some 800 to 1,100 miles and then no way to get back home. No moving expense, no nothing. So, he's just thrown out to fend for himself.*[47]

Further factoring into the increased call and need for African American labor from the South was the tightening of immigration laws culminating in the Emergency Immigration Act of 1921, which curtailed southern and eastern European immigration into America.[48] Much of this was a reaction to the Red Scare that was sweeping the country at the time in reaction to the Russian Revolution and the wave of Communist revolts and uprisings that were taking place in Europe. The backlash was nativist fear of foreign immigrants, as well as the burgeoning attempts of workers to unionize. The closing doors for European immigration opened new doors and needs for southern Blacks. Before this time, 90 percent of all African Americans in the United States lived below the Mason-Dixon line. Black workers made up less than 2 percent of all the steelworkers in the region. However, the reductions in European immigration, general employment demands brought on by the war and labor issues more than quintupled the number of African American workers in the region. By 1923, African American workers made up more than 20 percent of all the steelworkers in western Pennsylvania mills.[49] In Carnegie Steel's Homestead Works alone, the percentage of Black steelworkers rose from 1.8 percent in 1907 to 11.8 percent in 1919. The table below shows the percentage of workers by nationality from October 8, 1919. Of particular interest is how Black workers are designated—not as Americans, but in their own category.[50]

Nationality report, Homestead Steel Works, Howard Axle Works, Carrie Furnaces, Oct. 8, 1919.

Nationality	Number	Per cent.	Nationality	Number	Per cent.
American	5,799	39.45	Kreiner (Slovanian)	6	0.04
Armenian	15	.10	Lithuanian	238	1.62
Austrian	42	.29	Macedonian	4	.03
Arabian	5	.30	Mexican	130	.89
Albanian	25	.17	Negro:		
Austro-Servian	1	.01	American	1,734	11.80
Belgian	3	.02	British	1	.01
Bohemian	2	.01	East India	1	.01
Brazilian	1	.01	West India	1	.01
Bulgarian	67	.46	Norwegian	4	.03
Canadian	20	.14	Polish	432	2.94
Croatian (Horvat)	299	2.04	Portuguese	1	.01
Cuban	2	.01	Porto Rican	18	.12
Dalmatian	9	.06	Roumanian	49	.33
Danish	6	.04	Russian	628	4.28
English	424	2.89	Ruthenian	1	.01
Filipino	1	.01	Saxon	4	.03
Finnish	7	.05	Scotch	226	1.54
French	7	.05	Slovak	2,373	16.15
German	219	1.49	Servian	26	.18
Greek	267	1.82	Spanish	48	.33
Hebrew	11	.07	Swede	74	.50
Hindu	1	.01	Swiss	11	.07
Hollander	6	.04	Syrian	9	.06
Hungarian (Magyar)	574	3.91	Turk	53	.36
Indian	3	.02	Welsh	91	.62
Irish	443	3.02			
Italian	264	1.80	Total	14,687	100.6
Japanese	1	.01			

Report on the Steel Strike of 1919, Interchurch World Movement of North America. *Bureau of Industrial Research (New York: Harcourt, Brace and Howe, 1920).*

Blast furnace, coke and open-hearth plants became the domain of the Black steelworker. Labor gangs were dominated by African Americans, as were the worst of positions in the coke plants, rolling mills and furnaces. The Carrie Furnaces in Rankin and Swissvale after the 1930s were very typical of the era; 90 percent of the unskilled workforce was African American. There, they were exposed to the harshest of conditions, working with molten iron and slag coming from the furnaces. Most often, these workers were sent to the worst environments to toil for less pay and little representation. It was not until the consent decrees in the 1970s that the situation begrudgingly began to change—unfortunately, too late for many of the men who spent the previous thirty-plus years working in the worst of conditions. Herb Edwards remembered that so many Black people worked in the coke works because the white people were either placed in the steel mill or refused to work in the coke works. "I guess maybe only the blacks were capable or could stay on the job....Every man I looked at looked to be eighty years old when he was really young. I asked one man when he was going to retire, and he said, 'Retire? I'm forty-eight years old.'" When Herb walked out, he left everything behind—his pay, his clothes, everything. He did not even have another job to go to, nor did he care.[51]

Archie Coles, who worked for United States Steel Homestead Works for almost forty years, said his father was recruited from Virginia to work in the mills during the Great Migration. Archie followed his father into the mill and began working at the Homestead Works as a teenager before the end of World War II. While he eventually worked his way up to machinist, he endured many years of hard labor and dangerous conditions before he could advance in the industry.

> *Before the consent decree[52]...most of the jobs offered were labor gang, brick gang, narrow-gauge as hook ons. Very few decent jobs for Blacks. When I worked in the brick department, I had to deal with asbestos. We had the worst jobs...like a furnace would break down, the roof would cave in....We had to go on top of the roof with tongs and clear the roof. One time, Carrie Furnace had a big furnace that caved in, worked over there for three months. Had wooden shoes on...it was hot...very hot....Go in for 15 minutes then out for half an hour. Made maybe one dollar an hour, sometimes only 85 cents an hour.*
>
> *Sometimes in the labor gang—all the white guys would work on the loading dock on the wharf and the Black guys would have to go down into the barges and load the steel. No fire, nothing.*
>
> *Nothing happened until the consent decree came in. Took a while though....* [white] *folks weren't happy about it.*[53]

These stories of working in dangerous and often caustic conditions are repeated throughout most of the twentieth century. The worst of the jobs—the most backbreaking and hazardous—were reserved for African Americans. They had little choice and rarely were able to bid out of the labor gangs or furnace departments. Often, they found themselves among the last hired and the first fired—last in, first out. Employment, as with the work, was tenuous at best.

Cleaning runners at the Carrie Furnaces, circa 1940. *Courtesy of Rivers of Steel, Bowman Collection.*

Pulling scrap at the Carrie Furnaces, circa 1940. *Courtesy of Rivers of Steel, Bowman Collection.*

Pulling manganese at the Carrie Furnaces, circa 1940. *Courtesy of Rivers of Steel, Smerkel Collection.*

John Hughey continued:

> *And that particular time people—they would hire 20 in the morning, 15 would quit the same day and they would hire 20 more. They would only retain about five out of the 20 on the blast furnace. And that's the people that actually worked on the furnace front. And there's no training at that particular time. You learn what you want. And the accident rate was very high with burns and people getting hurt and falling out. They didn't even have salt tablets at that particular time to replenish your body. Somebody falls out, they just put him on the stretcher, take him to hospital, and put another man in their place back in '47.*
>
> *Well, Carrie was a particular place there, at that particular time when I come there, the maintenance department was 99—it was like Ivory Soap. It was 99 and 66, but pure of Caucasian. The furnace department, where the hard, dirty work was 99 percent Afro American or Black, or any term you want to use to describe Afro American. And at that particular time, Blacks were not allowed into maintenance or in the good, soft, paying jobs and trades and crafts and engineers and all that.*[54]

With the coming of the consent decree in 1974, overt corporation racism became illegal, and working conditions improved for many African

Homestead Steel Works Colored Club, 1938. *Courtesy of Rivers of Steel, Jane Alexander-Davis Collection.*

Americans working in the iron and steel industries. However, over the next ten years, the decline of the industry and deindustrialization set in. More than 150,000 men and women lost their jobs in manufacturing, which had fueled the region and the world for over 120 years. The layoffs were damaging to everyone—laborers and community members alike. The economic and social gains made during the previous decade were undone before they could even take hold.

However, the fabric of the region was forever shaped in a new and dynamic way by the Black steelworkers and their families who settled in the region in the late nineteenth and twentieth centuries. They came for improved economic and social conditions, some of which were achieved. Others remain elusive. The lessons of the past should not and cannot be lost on us. The difficulties that were, and still are, faced by Black Americans are important to be understood, remembered and celebrated—theirs is a story of survival, perseverance and pride.

Chapter 5

THE PROMISE AND LIMITS
OF OPPORTUNITIES FOR
AFRICAN AMERICANS, 1916–30

by Joe William Trotter Jr., Giant Eagle University Professor of History and
Social Justice, Carnegie Mellon University, and Current President of the
Urban History Association

As elsewhere across urban industrial America, the Great Migration transformed the economy, culture and politics of Pittsburgh and southwestern Pennsylvania during and following World War I. The vast majority of Black women continued to work in the low-wage household service sector of the expanding industrial economy, but African American men gained increasing access to jobs in the region's higher-paying steel, coal and coke plants. As their numbers dramatically increased, however, African American men and women faced stiff racial barriers on their socioeconomic mobility. Discriminatory labor, management, financial, real estate and municipal policies not only confined African Americans to the lower reaches of the occupational ladder but also limited their access to equal opportunities for livable housing, education and healthcare; leisure time and legal services; and justice before the law.

African Americans did not take the rise of Pittsburgh's segregationist order without a fight. Similar to their kinsmen and women across the nation's urban landscape, Black Pittsburgh built its own separate institutional, cultural and political infrastructure, challenging the emergence of the white supremacist order in cities and towns throughout southwestern Pennsylvania. As historian Earl Lewis so aptly described this process in Jim Crow Norfolk, Virginia, Afro-Pittsburgh transformed "segregation" into "congregation" and used their "city within the city" as a fortress against the destructive influence of the northern U.S. version of racial "apartheid."[55]

Under the impact of the Great Migration, Pittsburgh's African American population jumped by more than 100 percent between 1910 and 1930, rising from 25,600 to nearly 55,000. As early as 1917, the steel industry journal *Iron Age* reported trainloads of "Negroes bound from the South to Pittsburgh." Between 1915 and 1917 alone, over 18,000 African Americans moved to the Steel City. Whereas Virginia, Maryland, the District of Columbia and other Upper South and border states dominated the Black migration stream to Pittsburgh before World War I, thereafter, increasing numbers of war and postwar Blacks came to Pittsburgh from the cotton-producing states of Georgia, South Carolina, Mississippi and Alabama. While some of these young men soon enlisted in the armed forces, most added their labor to the city and region's industrial workforce.[56]

Rising numbers of Black men obtained jobs at the U.S. Steel Homestead Works, Jones and Laughlin Steel and Carnegie Steel, among other leading industrial employers. Some of these men had worked in the steel, coke and coal industries of the urban South. "I came here from Birmingham," one migrant later recalled. "I spent the better part of my life there.... Pittsburgh wasn't strange. It was like Birmingham. They're both mineral towns."[57] But others entered Pittsburgh more directly from rural farming and agricultural environments. Unlike their urban-industrial counterparts, the process of steelmaking amazed these newcomers. As one rural migrant put it, "All [the steel] I had seen in previous years was all finished and hard and everything. To come [to Pittsburgh] and see it running like water—it was very amazing." The cotton "South is clean," these rural farm and plantation migrants also said. "Everything is white, beautiful....Everything was black and smoky here."[58]

Notwithstanding the city's unhealthy geography, migrants nonetheless celebrated the opening of job opportunities and higher wages in the industrial sector compared to their southern homes. In Pittsburgh, Black men earned over $3.50 per eight-hour day compared to only $2.50 per twelve-hour day in southern cities and only about $1.00 per day as farm laborers. By the late 1920s, the Pennsylvania Department of Welfare reported that the net family earnings of migrant Black workers averaged 70 percent higher (despite higher costs of living in the urban North) than in the South. Given these improvements in earning capacity, some migrants understandably described their arrival in the industrial city in such biblical terms as the "Promised Land," "New Jerusalem" and escape "from Egypt."[59]

Blast furnace and stoves. *Reprinted in John A. Fitch,* The Steel Workers, *courtesy University of Pittsburgh Press.*

Alongside the vigorous labor recruitment efforts of area steel firms and coal mines, African Americans forged their own kinship and communal networks and shaped their own movement into the industrial city. Black women emerged at the dynamic center of this migration network. One migrant's wife highlighted the influence of African American women on patterns of Black migration when she penned a letter to the Urban League of Pittsburgh on behalf of herself and her two sons. I have "two grown sons," she said. "We want to settle down somewhere in the north....Wages are so cheap down here we can hardly live." At about the same time, another woman implored her husband to leave Cincinnati and secure a job in Pittsburgh. "My older sister had come to Pittsburgh, and I took her as a mother because I had lost my mother....I don't want to stay in Cincinnati. I want to go to Pittsburgh....Next letter I got, he had got a job in Pittsburgh and sent for me."[60]

Despite experiencing a degree of upward economic mobility, African American life and labor was not easy in Pittsburgh. Steelmaking was a hazardous, health- and life-threatening occupation for all steelworkers across ethnic and racial lines. But Black people endured the lion's share of dangerous and unhealthy jobs on blast furnaces. Divided between "front" and "back" workers, African Americans took the bulk of the most arduous back-end occupations: the most difficult, hot and dirty work hauling the "molten iron and slag."[61] They also crawled into certain areas of the blast furnaces "to clean out dust and soot." Lethal fumes and deadly heat sometimes reached "over 2,000 degrees Fahrenheit." One furnace hand later vividly recalled hazards of the work—how "first you get a headache, and the stomach bothers you and then you have to come out....Colored are given this type of work mostly."[62] In 1919, African Americans made up nearly 5 percent of all the state's iron, steel and manufacturing workers, but they composed almost 10 percent of all victims of industrial accidents.[63]

Discriminatory employment and labor policies ensured that African Americans not only occupied lower-end jobs but also that they earned less for "doing the same job" as white workers. A comparative study of twelve industrial sector jobs in the urban North, including Pittsburgh, revealed that whites earned an estimated 20 percent higher wages than Blacks performing similar work. Black women also gradually gained jobs in the industrial sector of the economy. But the percentage of Black women in household work dropped only slightly from about 88 to 86 percent. Much like Black men, however, pioneering Black female industrial workers entered the most difficult job classifications in only a few firms, most significantly the National Shirt Factory and the Lockhart Iron and Steel Company.[64]

African Americans devised a variety of strategies for changing the terms on which they lived and worked. In the Great Steel Strike of 1919 and the coal strikes of the mid-1920s, they boldly crossed the picket lines of racially exclusionary white labor unions. In the steel strike, one Black strikebreaker declared, "All I am interested in is to make a living…and no 'hunky' has a right to keep me from working." Likewise, in the coal strike of 1927, a Black miner reminded striking white workers of their discriminatory practices before the strike. "You would not work with me before the strike. Now I have your job and I am going to keep it." "The time to beg is past!" another Black worker said. "We must assert ourselves and demand our rights! My father was a slave, but his son won't be one!"[65]

As Pittsburgh's Black industrial working class expanded during the Great Migration, African Americans faced increasing restriction on where they could live, educate their children and receive necessary healthcare and social services. The city's realtors, homeowners and banks resisted the movement of African Americans into all-white neighborhoods. African Americans gained homes in a few racially segregated communities across southwestern Pennsylvania, including Homestead, Braddock, Duquesne and Johnstown, as well as Pittsburgh. During World War I, only about 13 percent of African

Wooden tenements in the Hill District on the eve of the Great Migration in 1914. *Courtesy of Archives and Special Collections, University of Pittsburgh Library System.*

Americans owned their own homes, compared to an estimated 50 percent for Euro-American families.[66]

The largest concentration of African Americans emerged in Pittsburgh's Hill District. With substantial vacancies in low-rent white areas, Pittsburgh realtors and homeowners nonetheless excluded African American tenants. Instead, they converted railroad cars, basements, boathouses and warehouses into living quarters for Black workers and their families, while steel companies housed single men in segregated makeshift camps. Black migrants often occupied overcrowded rooms with two, three or four men to a single bed, often sleeping on double shifts at the height of the Great Migration. By the onset of the Great Depression, the vast majority of Pittsburgh's Black population occupied segregated, dilapidated and deteriorating homes. They nonetheless paid much higher rents for shabby dwellings than their white counterparts for comparable quarters. In 1926, according to a local banking firm's report, Black residents paid nearly 25 percent of their total earnings for rent. By contrast, white families paid only 7 percent of their wages for rental housing.[67]

In the face of major obstacles and roadblocks to their quest for better housing, African Americans gradually increased their rate of homeownership and access to better homes from no more than 10 percent at the outset of World War I to about 17 percent in 1930. They gained their most notable opportunities for homeownership in the Upper Hill District. Citywide, however, a small number of Black professional and businesspeople, like Robert L. Vann, and their families represented a disproportionate share of Black homeowners, but homeowners also included poor and working-class Black residents, like the general laborer James Coleman and his wife, Lucy. In 1923, the Colemans purchased a lot at 845 Perry Street. They took out a mortgage on the land, retired the mortgage in 1925 and took out "two new mortgages…to build a two-story brick veneer house."[68]

The color line did not stop at the boundaries of the labor and housing markets. Jim Crow crisscrossed every aspect of the city's institutional and cultural life. Downtown restaurants, department stores, hotels, theaters and schools either excluded or segregated African Americans. Moreover, on a day-to-day basis, racial hostility greeted African Americans in public spaces, as symbolized by the spread of local chapters of the Ku Klux Klan across Pittsburgh and southwestern Pennsylvania. Membership in local and regional Klaverns increased to more than 120,000 during the early 1920s. In 1925, when the national Klan staged a rally at the nation's capital, Pittsburgh-area Klansmen claimed the largest number of delegates attending the event.[69]

In December 1920, authorities arrested and charged Joe Thomas with the murder of Anna Kirker, a white woman, in a place called Buttermilk Bottom in nearby Mifflin Township. The only tangible clue in the case was footprints outside the woman's home, but the footprints matched those of her husband. Even so, there was a great public outcry to find the killer before authorities fully queried Kirker's spouse. Nearly two months later, police wounded a Black man, presumably a bootlegger, Joe Thomas, in an unrelated gun battle. Upon searching the accused, police reported finding the victim's watch. Authorities later convicted Thomas of murder and sentenced him to death on flimsy or even fabricated evidence.[70]

After a brief escape from custody before his trial and execution, Thomas moved to Baltimore, where he was later apprehended and returned to Pittsburgh. The mayor of the city and some one thousand white residents met the train that brought Thomas back to the city. Thomas died in the electric chair in December 1922. The white newspapers repeatedly called him the "Ape Man." Thomas repeatedly proclaimed his innocence. Just before his execution, he said, "I am not afraid to die, but I hate to go to the

Joe Thomas, the southern newcomer to Pittsburgh accused, tried and sentenced to death for the alleged murder of a white woman in 1922. *Courtesy of the* Pittsburgh Post-Gazette.

electric chair with people calling me an ape man....If the people who send me to the chair are ready to meet their God, I am ready to meet mine."[71]

Against the hostile backdrop of racial injustice in the city and region, as elsewhere across urban industrial America, African Americans built their own "city within the city." They transformed "segregation," a mean-spirited separation of the races, into "congregation," a dynamic process of community building to address their own needs in the Jim Crow social order. They established an expanding array of churches, fraternal orders, women's clubs and business and professional services to meet the demands for services among their own people. They also used their expanding "Black metropolis," as it was also frequently called, to launch energetic grassroots social and political movements to both combat and demolish the white supremacist Jim Crow order. Local chapters of national Black organizations emerged at the center of these movements, including, most notably, Pittsburgh branches of the National Association for the Advancement of Colored People (NAACP), the National Urban League (NUL), the National Association of Colored Women (NACW) and the Universal Negro Improvement Association (UNIA) or Garvey Movement.[72]

Despite a remarkable display of racial solidarity and unity, African American community formation and freedom movements encountered significant internal fragmentation and conflicts along ideological, class and gender lines. From the outset of the Great Migration, southern Blacks confronted hostility from old residents who claimed deep roots in the early nineteenth century. "Old Pittsburghers," as they were called, believed the newcomers threatened to disrupt what they perceived as relatively amicable relations between Blacks and whites. At the same time, organizations like the Urban League of Pittsburgh (ULP) launched vigorous campaigns to

Considered the "crossroads of the world," Wylie Avenue in the Hill District, facing west, April 1930. *Courtesy of Archives and Special Collections, University of Pittsburgh Library System.*

transform the culture of southern Blacks, particularly poor and working-class southerners.

The ULP as well as leading Black ministers hoped to curtail the leisure time activities of migrants, particularly gambling, the consumption of strong drinks and the shouting tradition in religious services. Moreover, southern Black migrants fueled the popular growth of the Garvey Movement with its emphasis on "Race First" over the NAACP and Urban League's abiding interest in building interracial coalitions designed to erase the color line from all facets of the urban environment. At the same time, although African American women played a key role not only in migration networks but also in the institution-building and political organizing work of the African American community, they confronted entrenched male resistance to their full enfranchisement within Black organizations like the church and the fraternal orders. Stiff gender conventions prevented their entrance into the ministry as preachers.

By the onset of the Great Depression, African Americans had enriched the predominantly white city through their labor. Within the context of ongoing cleavages and social conflicts within their own community, they

Above: The 22 Crosstown streetcar recognizes "44 years of American teamwork" by the Urban League, a national civil rights and urban advocacy organization. *Courtesy of Archives and Special Collections, University of Pittsburgh Library System.*

Left: Marchers pass near the Civic Arena as they make their way from the Hill District to Downtown via Centre Avenue three days after the assassination of Dr. Martin Luther King Jr. *Courtesy of Archives and Special Collections, University of Pittsburgh Library System.*

had also successfully channeled their meager resources into the building of their own "Black metropolis." Replete with its own dynamic institutional infrastructure, the Black city not only served the day-to-day social service, spiritual and health needs of the African American community, but it also provided the foundation for mobilizing against racial apartheid and demanding equal rights and social justice for all citizens in Pittsburgh, southwestern Pennsylvania and the nation.

Chapter 6

GUS GREENLEE

A Racketeer on the Move

by Mark Whitaker, author of *Smoketown: The Untold Story of the Other Great Black Renaissance*

On April 29, 1932, the Black community of Pittsburgh enjoyed a rare day of celebration in one of the darkest years of the Great Depression.[73] Thousands of spectators flocked to the corner of Bedford Avenue and Junilla Street in the Hill District to watch the first baseball game played in Greenlee Field. The ballpark was named after the man who had built it: Pittsburgh's leading Black racketeer, Gus Greenlee, a tall, burly man with thinning red hair and a freckled moon face that could shift in an instant from an intimidating scowl to a jovial smile. After buying a local sandlot baseball team called the Pittsburgh Crawfords, "Big Red," as Greenlee was known around town,[74] was said to have spent no less than $100,000 to construct a stadium as part of his bid to turn the upstart Crawfords into a powerhouse in the Negro Leagues.

The game that day, between the Crawfords and the visiting New York Black Yankees, was preceded by an elaborate dedication ceremony. A band marched onto the field and played "The Star-Spangled Banner." Robert L. Vann, the ambitious publisher who was on his way to turning the *Pittsburgh Courier* into the best-read Black newspaper in America, gave a speech. Then Vann introduced the man of the hour. As everyone in the stands rose to their feet and craned their necks, a bright red Packard convertible drove onto the field carrying Gus Greenlee in the back seat—

Gus Greenlee with an unnamed woman at the Crawford Grill about 1943. *Charles "Teenie" Harris Archive/Carnegie Museum of Art via Getty Images.*

Although a later model, this candy-apple red 1938 Packard Twelve is similar to the car Gus Greenlee rode onto the field on the Pittsburgh Crawfords' opening day in 1932. *Courtesy the Auburn Cord Duesenberg Automobile Museum, Auburn, Indiana.*

From 1931 to 1935, Buick offered the exclusivity and refinement found in luxury brands like Packard with the Series 90 line. Unlike the "flashy" Cadillac, the Series 90 displayed a muted elegance while maintaining Buick's reputation for durability and reliability. *Courtesy The NB Center for American Automotive Heritage.*

his ample frame sheathed in a white silk suit and a Cuban cigar dangling from his mouth as he waved to the appreciative crowd.

In those days, everyone in Black Pittsburgh knew Gus Greenlee,[75] and everyone recognized his cars. Greenlee was the city's top Black "numbers runner," overseeing a daily gambling operation—a precursor to today's national and state lotteries—in which thousands of hopeful betters spent hard-earned dimes and dollars to pick a combination of numbers in hopes of winning a big payout. But he was more than that. Like other top Black racketeers in cities across America during the Great Depression, Gus had also become a business entrepreneur, a political fixer and a community banker of last resort. To make his power and wealth visible on the Hill, Greenlee drove to work each day from his home—a spacious Tudor house in the wealthy town of Penn Hills northeast of the city—in one of six expensive vehicles: a Lincoln, a Cadillac, a Chevy, a Buick, a Ford or the dashing red Packard convertible.

From an early age, Greenlee viewed trains and automobiles as means not only of getting around but also of getting ahead.[76] He was born in Marion, North Carolina, a mill town at the base of the Blue Ridge Mountains, to a relatively prosperous Black family. His father was a masonry contractor who had made a handsome sum when he was hired to rebuild some of Marion's leading white business establishments after they were destroyed by fire. His mother, the offspring of an enslaved Black woman and her white owner, stressed the value of education to all her children. Two of the Greenlee sons became lawyers and another a doctor. But Gus was an indifferent student with a rebellious streak who got "on the dogs with father," as he described the family clashes. At the age of nineteen, after finishing only one year of college, he hopped a hobo ride on a train headed to Pittsburgh, carrying nothing more than a few days' worth of clothing and wearing canvas shoes that he soon discovered would not take him far in the harsh winters of western Pennsylvania.

The year was 1912, just as the Great Migration was gathering steam, an exodus that would eventually bring six million Black people from the South to the North.[77] Like many of the migrants to Pittsburgh, Greenlee looked for a job in the city's steel plants. He found one, but he wasn't content simply to work for meager wages under the eyes of white factory foremen. On the side, he shined shoes and got a job as a chauffeur for a white funeral home owner. That gave Greenlee the idea of operating his own taxi service, and he saved up his money until he could buy a cab. He held onto the vehicle even after enlisting to fight in World War I and serving as a machine gunner with a Buffalo Soldiers unit in France, where he suffered a shrapnel wound while under the command of General John Pershing in the Meuse-Argonne Offensive.

Shortly after the war ended and Greenlee returned to Pittsburgh, the Wartime Prohibition Act was passed on July 1, 1919—otherwise known as "June thirsty-first." It was the first step toward Prohibition, the 1920 constitutional amendment banning all production, transportation and sales of liquor in the United States. Suddenly, Greenlee's taxicab had a new use.[78] Four Italian American racketeers known as the Tito brothers started a beer-and whiskey-making operation in Latrobe, the small city south of Pittsburgh that would later become famous as the birthplace of golfer Arnold Palmer and home of Rolling Rock beer. The Tito brothers hired Greenlee to distribute their illicit wares across the region, and soon he was logging so many miles that he earned the nickname "Gasoline Gus."

Bootlegging quickly became a very dangerous business, however, as mob bosses such as Al Capone and Lucky Luciano staged armed hijackings of one another's trucks and went gunning for anyone who tried to muscle in on their turf. With a shrewd mixture of cunning and caution, Greenlee took his rumrunning proceeds and branched out into less perilous enterprises. He purchased a hotel called the Paramount in the Hill District and converted it first into a speakeasy and then a nightclub. Next, he turned his attention to numbers running, which had also arrived in Pittsburgh in the early 1920s via the railroad. Madame Stephanie St. Clair, known as the "Policy Queen of Harlem," hired Black Pullman porters to take bets on stops along their train routes between New York and other cities. ("Policy" was another name for the numbers game, a sly reference to gambling as a poor man's insurance policy.)

Woogie Harris with Lena Horne in the years she lived in Pittsburgh. Her father, Teddy Horne, was a numbers runner like Harris. *Charles "Teenie" Harris Archive/Carnegie Museum of Art via Getty Images.*

After watching a local Black doctor who tried to start a numbers operations in Pittsburgh go broke, Greenlee proceeded with care. He looked for a popular figure on the Hill who could serve as a "cut buddy" to share risks and rewards. He chose William Harris, known to everyone in the neighborhood as "Woogie," the well-liked owner of the Crystal Barber Shop on Wylie Avenue in the Hill District.[79] As their numbers operation expanded, Woogie turned the back room of the barbershop into a counting office. While men with guns hidden under their topcoats stood guard on the street and barbers cut hair and lathered whiskers in front of the ornate paneled mirrors inside, numbers runners dropped off bags of money and gambling slips at the back door, and a staff of women tallied the day's take on adding machines.

One of the first runners Greenlee and Harris put to work was Woogie's younger brother Charles, known to everyone as "Teenie."[80] (People assumed that the younger Harris had acquired that nickname because he

The Crystal Barbershop in the Hill District, behind which Gus and Woogie ran their numbers counting operation. *Charles "Teenie" Harris Archive/Carnegie Museum of Art via Getty Images.*

was short in stature, but in fact, it originated with his good looks: when he was a child, smitten older women dubbed him "Teenie Little Lover.") For Teenie, collecting bets gave him the chance to indulge his own passion for cars. As soon as he was old enough to drive, he advertised himself as a "chauffeur" in the local phone book. For a time, he drove hand-me-downs from Woogie. But then Teenie became a photographer and grew so successful that he could afford his own fancy wheels. He opened a portrait studio on the Hill and became a staff photographer for the *Courier*, a job that allowed him to capture every aspect of Black life in Pittsburgh over the next half a century. Looking back on their childhoods, Teenie's children remembered how much their father coveted each new model of the luxury Cadillacs, bodies custom-built in Fleetwood, Pennsylvania, and how he knew the streets of Pittsburgh so well that he could get anywhere in the city without encountering traffic lights.

In August 1930, just as their numbers operation was taking off, Greenlee and Woogie went on vacation and left Teenie in charge.[81] At the time,

Teenie Harris with two loves: his Speed Graphic camera and his 1940 Cadillac. *Charles "Teenie" Harris Archive/Carnegie Museum of Art via Getty Images.*

the racketeers set the daily odds at 600-to-1, and they based the winning three-digit numbers on the next day's stock tables—combining the last digits of the numbers of stocks that went up, went down and stayed even. On the fifth day of the month, a brutal heat wave left hundreds of Black Pittsburghers so tired that the only number they could think to play was the date: 805. When the number "hit" the next day, tens of thousands of dollars in payouts were owed. Teenie reached Woogie in Europe with the news, and Woogie gave him an address where he could go to get $25,000 in cash with no questions asked. Then Greenlee and Woogie rushed back to Pittsburgh and took out new mortgages on their houses in Penn Hills to pay off the rest of the gamblers. Meanwhile, other numbers runners skipped town, allowing those who hung on to expand their turfs. One vanished white racketeer became the subject of a sarcastic ditty: "805 was a burner. Where the hell is Jackie Lerner?"

In the following years, Greenlee reached the height of his influence in Black Pittsburgh.[82] He purchased another hotel known as the Leader House and turned it into a nightclub called the Crawford Grill. On the first floor, he installed a long bar with a mirror-covered piano perched on top. On the second floor was a theater with a stage; on the third, a private club where Greenlee entertained business associates and famous celebrities and athletes who passed through Pittsburgh. After performing at the Stanley Theater downtown, the likes of Duke Ellington and Cab Calloway made their way to the third floor of Crawford Grill and stayed to drink and socialize until the wee hours. Allying himself with the Republican political machine that ran the city, Greenlee became the head of the Third Ward Voter's League, telling Black folk on the Hill which candidates to support and helping get them to the polls on election day. In turn, city officials looked away from Greenlee's illegal activities—or tipped him off in advance when they occasionally staged a token raid for the benefit of the newspapers.

As the Great Depression deepened, Pittsburgh's white-run banks stopped dispensing money of any kind to the city's Black residents, and Greenlee became the community's de facto banker. He doled out loans to cover rents, to prevent mortgage foreclosures and to pay for weddings and funerals. When breadwinners got laid off from jobs in Pittsburgh's steel mills and other factories, Greenlee gave them temporary jobs in his numbers operation. Around the holidays, he sent bags of groceries and truckloads of coal to families in distress. To make sure that everyone on the Hill heard about his generosity, he put one of the city's best-known journalists on his personal payroll. John L. Clark was the author of "Wylie Avenue," the *Courier*'s gossip column about life on the Hill. When Greenlee got word that Clark planned a story about racketeering, he invited him for a drink at the Crawford Grill. Clark never wrote that column and instead started serving as Greenlee's publicist, turning the "Wylie Avenue" column into a source of updates on Greenlee's political influence and financial largesse.

Greenlee's most famous act of generosity came when the Pittsburgh Crawfords sandlot baseball team went looking for an investor.[83] The team had been formed by graduates of two rival high school teams, one of whom was Teenie Harris. By the early 1930s, the "Craws," as they were known, had become a big attraction on the Hill—mostly because of their catcher and star slugger, a husky teenager named Josh Gibson with a devastatingly compact and powerful swing. But the city would not allow the team to charge for attendance at the public ballfield where they played, so they could barely afford uniforms and equipment. After *Courier* sportswriter Chester Washington wrote a column pleading the Crawfords' cause, the white owner of a local sporting goods store offered to sponsor them. But

The Pittsburgh Crawfords during their spring training in Hot Springs, Arkansas, 1932. Satchel Paige and Josh Gibson are second and third from the left in the back row. *Transcendental Graphics/Getty Images.*

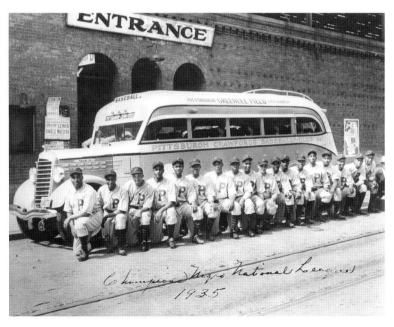

Considered the greatest team in the history of the Negro Leagues, the 1935 Crawfords, with four future hall of famers—Josh Gibson, Oscar Charleston, Judy Johnson and Cool Papa Bell—went 51-26-3 overall, winning the Negro National League's championship series. *Courtesy the National Baseball Hall of Fame and Museum.*

instead, the players approached Gus Greenlee. After initially resisting, he offered to purchase the team outright.

At the time, Pittsburgh had one Negro League team: the Homestead Grays. They were managed and later owned by Cumberland "Cum" Posey Jr., who came from one of the wealthiest Black families in the area. Just as Greenlee was buying the Crawfords, Posey hired Josh Gibson away to play for the Grays. Greenlee retaliated by benching most of the other sandlot players and assembling a team that would outshine his crosstown rivals. He acquired legendary pitcher Satchel Paige when the Cleveland team Paige was playing for went bankrupt. Greenlee enticed Gibson back with a higher offer a day after Posey had re-signed him. He also stole two more of the Grays' top players—first baseman Oscar Charleston and third baseman Judy Johnson—and signed the fastest base runner in the Negro Leagues, "Cool Papa" Bell.

Greenlee also marketed the Crawfords in a way the Pittsburgh sports world had never seen before.[84] In addition to building the team their own ballpark—Greenlee Field—he organized spring training tours of the South, where the Craws played top Black sandlot teams and white exhibition squads. He bought a huge tour bus and had the Pittsburgh Crawfords logo painted in huge letters on the side, then sent reporter John L. Clark along to send back photographs and glowing reports of the road trip to the *Courier*. During the 1932 and 1933 seasons, the Crawfords lived up to the hype by amassing the best win-loss record in the Negro Leagues. Just as satisfying to Greenlee, they also regularly beat Cum Posey's Homestead Grays in head-to-head series.

As the decade continued, however, Greenlee's luck started to run out.[85] He feuded with the mercenary Satchel Paige, who kept leaving the Crawfords for better offers. He suffered financial losses promoting a boxer named John Henry Lewis and was said to have also faced big numbers payouts that he didn't weather as well as the 805 crisis. Greenlee Field also turned out to be far less lucrative than he had hoped, both because the lack of a roof kept fans away on hot or rainy days and because Greenlee had awarded the concession business to the Tito brothers. Meanwhile, Cum Posey found a racketeer of his own to help bankroll the Grays—a Homestead numbers runner known as "Sonnyman" Jackson. By the late 1930s, Greenlee was forced to close Greenlee Field and sell the land to the government for a new public housing project, and he no longer had the wherewithal to compete when Posey made offers to woo Josh Gibson and the other top Crawford players back to the Grays.

Before long, Gus Greenlee's fall was followed by the overall demise of the beneficent inner-city numbers game as he had known it. After World War II, ambitious white politicians stepped up racketeering investigations, and middle-class whites and Blacks fled to the suburbs. Eventually, states and cities launched their own lotteries, with far less direct benefit to urban communities. The Negro Leagues went into decline, too, once the long-overdue integration of Major League baseball began in 1947 when Jackie Robinson joined the Brooklyn Dodgers.

Although largely unremembered, Greenlee played an important minor role in that historical development as well.[86] In the 1930s, he originated a Black all-star baseball game called the East-West Classic that gave white sportswriters and fans a taste of the base-stealing, acrobatic-fielding excitement that Black players could bring to the Major Leagues. Then, in the mid-1940s, Greenlee briefly tried to get back into baseball by forming a new Black league called the United States League. When he approached Dodgers general manager Branch Rickey about renting out Ebbets Field, a dialogue began that led to Rickey scouting and signing Robinson, then a rookie for the Kansas City Monarchs of the Negro Leagues.

On July 7, 1952, the remarkable personal journey that had begun in rural North Carolina ended when Gus Greenlee died of a stroke in Pittsburgh at the age of fifty-seven. In the pages of the *Courier*, Wendell Smith—the famed sportswriter who served as Rickey's go-between to Jackie Robinson—captured the essence of Greenlee's individual legacy and the collective esteem in which Black racketeers of his era were held within their communities: not as criminals, but as champions of the race.[87] Concluding his eulogy, Smith wrote admiringly: "Greenlee was interested in fostering the advancement of Negro players, no matter what it cost him personally. He was a big man physically and spiritually....He was the kind of man you should never forget."

Chapter 7

DESTINATION: APPLE STREET

by Jonnet Solomon, Executive Director, National Negro Opera House

The big Queen Anne–style house sitting high on the hill at 7101 Apple Street commands attention. Intricate details, colorful paint, unique windows and a towering turret make this complex structure iconic. Its mesmerizing beauty is communicated through the asymmetrical design and wraparound porch. The eyes are easily deceived by the detailed stucco work that imitates stone. Visitors are mesmerized by the intricate lattice surrounding the front door, crafted by skilled carpenters. Yet the beauty of the house is transcended by the energy of the souls—still felt today—who walked through the doors of this magnificent structure when it was home to the National Negro Opera Company.

HOW DID APPLE STREET BECOME A DESTINATION?

Apple Street is in Lincoln-Lemington-Belmar, a neighborhood in northeast Pittsburgh that spans the Allegheny River. This street sits on a steep hill that overlooks the city and connects to Lincoln Avenue and Upland Street. The neighborhood was white from the early 1920s until the 1970s, when it transitioned to a Black neighborhood. When William "Woogie" Harris purchased the house in the 1940s, he was the only African American

Owned by William "Woogie" Harris (1896–1967), the house at 7101 Apple Street in Pittsburgh's Homewood neighborhood was the headquarters of the National Negro Opera Company established by Mary Cardwell Dawson in 1942. *Charles "Teenie" Harris Archive/ Carnegie Museum of Art via Getty Images.*

homeowner on Apple Street. He fashioned 7101 Apple Street into a must-stop destination for musicians, artists, athletes and wealthy businesspeople—not just locals but also travelers and new arrivals from the South.

Upon arrival, visitors were greeted by admirable cars parked along Apple Street in front of the house, creating a magnificent display of wealth and prosperity. Pittsburgh entrepreneurs Woogie and Teenie Harris were known to have very nice cars, which they were proud to keep clean and fresh. The cars of visiting celebrities were also part of the scene. This remarkable sight was inspiring for Black residents and visitors because purchasing a car was very difficult for a Black person; for many, it was impossible. Philanthropists such as Gus Greenlee and Woogie Harris were valuable assets to the community because they funded car purchases and served as the informal "bank" for the Black community. This gave people the mobility they needed to access jobs, earn more money and build wealth.

Purchasing a car was only the first step in the adventure of Black car owners. Traveling by car took courage and tenacity. In a time with no GPS,

Seen here with a 1927 Cadillac LaSalle, entrepreneur Woogie Harris and his partner, William "Gus" Greenlee, became two of Pittsburgh's wealthiest racketeers. Harris was Pittsburgh's first Black millionaire. *Carnegie Museum of Art, Pittsburgh, Charles "Teenie" Harris Archive, 1996.90.38.*

Right: This intimate, informal mid-1930s photograph of Woogie Harris and son on Harris's luxury Duesenberg automobile was likely only possible because the photographer, Charles "Teenie" Harris, was his brother. *Charles "Teenie" Harris Archive/Carnegie Museum of Art via Getty Images.*

Below: Teenie Harris (1908–1998), the renowned photographer for the *Pittsburgh Courier*, is best known for documenting Pittsburgh's historic African American community. This photo shows the photographer and his son, Charles "Little Teenie" Harris, with a 1938 Cadillac in the driveway of his brother Woogie Harris's house on Frankstown Road, Penn Hills, about 1940. *Carnegie Museum of Art, Pittsburgh, Heinz Family Fund, Charles "Teenie" Harris Archive, 2001.35.6199.*

phone or modern highway system, getting into a car to go anywhere was not for the faint of heart. Furthermore, getting into a car while Black could be a death sentence. Making the journey to 7101 Apple Street—locally or nationally—posed potential hazards because few laws protected civil rights, and even fewer were enforced. Even so, many believed the risky trip to the house was a journey worth taking.

What gave these pilgrims the desire and courage to travel to Apple Street? What pushed them through the twists and turns, the steep uphills and downhills, the sharp curves and unpaved roads until they reached 7101? What made them stick it out, not give up and see that success is on the other side of failure?

The audacity of making the road trip as a Black woman or man—alone or in a group—was rewarded with a badge of survival, a community of like minds and the warmth, love and energy of high spirits emanating from the big house on Apple Street that can still be felt today. As the home of the National Negro Opera Company, it was an important and impressive cultural hub for African Americans in its day. The story of the opera company's founding and evolution reveals why it was so important to Pittsburgh's Black community.

Pittsburgh was called capitalism's first city. It was a principal urban symbol of America's industrial might. Some of the nation's wealthiest people lived in Pittsburgh, including the country's Black elite. Everyone knew where the society crowd gathered: the Loendi Club, private clubs and the National Negro Opera Company on Apple Street.

The National Negro Opera Company (NNOC), founded by Madame Mary Lucinda Cardwell Dawson, was the first Black opera company in America. The opportunities and access it offered were so valuable and unique that pushing through the challenges of getting there seemed trivial. Students arriving at the house never knew what adventure they might have or what celebrity, sports athlete or business tycoon they would encounter.

Mary Lucinda Cardwell was born on February 14, 1894, to James and Elizabeth Cardwell in Madison, North Carolina, one of six children born of that union. Mary lived with her parents and siblings in Madison until the family moved to Munhall, Pennsylvania, when she was seven years old. At an early age, Mary showed musical talent and promise beginning with first singing in her church choir and then extending to the piano, organ and conducting. Her talent was nurtured by her family, who encouraged Mary to enroll in Boston's New England Conservatory of Music, where she was the only African American in her class. To finance her education, she took

Above: The Loendi Social & Literary Club was an exclusive African American organization located in the Lower Hill District. Founded by George Hall in 1897, the Loendi offered lectures, musical performances and a quiet meeting place for the area's Black movers and shakers to do business. Photographer Teenie Harris captured the scene there in 1938. *Carnegie Museum of Art, Pittsburgh, Heinz Family Fund, Charles "Teenie" Harris Archive, 2001.35.39649.*

Left: Mary Cardwell Dawson (1894–1962) established NNOC to provide opportunities for gifted African Americans. She also challenged racist ideas by using white orchestras and conductors to accompany Black opera casts. *Library of Congress, Music Division. National Negro Opera Company.*

Ahmad Jamal, praised as a great jazz pioneer, was born in Pittsburgh in 1930. Jamal studied piano from age seven under the tutelage of Mary Cardwell Dawson and credits his innovative sound to his Pittsburgh roots. *JP Jazz Archive via Getty Images.*

a job cleaning a dentist's office. In 1925, at age thirty-one, she graduated with degrees in voice and piano and then continued her studies at the Chicago Musical College and in New York with aspirations to begin a career in opera.

While studying in Boston, Mary Cardwell met Walter Dawson. The couple courted, fell in love and were married on June 24, 1927. Not long after their marriage, the Dawsons returned to Pennsylvania and moved to Homestead to begin a life at 146 East 20th Street. Discrimination and racism might have prevented her from achieving her goal of becoming an opera singer, but those same roadblocks opened her eyes to the need to create opportunities for herself. Spurred on by the inequality, Mary Cardwell Dawson founded the Cardwell Dawson School of Music and opened a rehearsal space above her husband's electrical company service shop on Frankstown Road in East Liberty. From this space, she gave music lessons. One of her most accomplished students was Ahmad Jamal, who became a jazz pianist, composer, bandleader and educator. For over six decades, he was the most successful small group leader of jazz Pittsburgh has ever known.

She directed a choir of five hundred singers, sourced from local churches, which won national awards in 1935 and 1937. The students from her school of music (including two of her siblings, Harold and Catherine) became the Cardwell Dawson Choir. Nationally known for their excellence, the choir toured the country through the late 1930s, performing at the Century of Progress Exposition in Chicago and at the New York World's Fair in 1939.

The acclaim of the Cardwell Dawson Choir resulted in her nomination to the presidency of the National Association of Negro Musicians (NANM) in 1938. At the NANM annual conference, Dawson was asked to produce an opera, Verdi's *Aida*, with a cast of African American singers whom she selected through an audition process from the ten states represented at the conference that year. The success of this production and the acclaim that followed inspired her—now called Madame Cardwell Dawson, in proper opera fashion—to create an opera company to offer opportunities to

Above: This broadside is from the National Negro Opera Company's October 1954 production of Verdi's *Aida* at the Syria Mosque in Pittsburgh. The first time Cardwell Dawson produced *Aida*, in 1941, the public acclaim convinced her to found a Black opera company and provide opportunities denied by racism in the opera world. *Mary Cardwell Dawson Papers, Detre Library & Archives/Heinz History Center.*

Opposite, top: The 1954 NNOC production of *Aida*, staged at Soldiers and Sailors Memorial Hall, received a glowing review in the *Pittsburgh Courier* in which P.L. Prattis declared, "It wasn't simply 'good for Negroes' opera. It was a show that might have roused Verdi himself....You must see and hear this opera." *Charles "Teenie" Harris Archive/Carnegie Museum of Art via Getty Images.*

Opposite, bottom: The well-attended NNOC performance of *La Traviata* at Pittsburgh's Syria Mosque in January 1944 featured lyric soprano Lillian Evanti, well known in Europe, in the role of Violetta. Pittsburgher Joseph Lipscomb played the role of Alfredo. *Charles "Teenie" Harris Archive/Carnegie Museum of Art via Getty Images.*

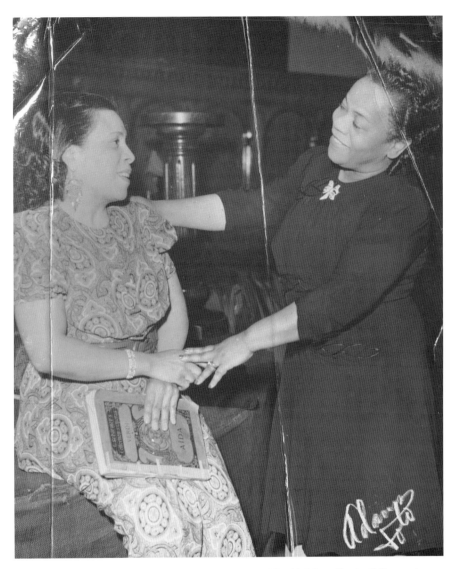

American operatic soprano La Julia Rhea (1898–1992, *left*, with Mary Cardwell Dawson) starred in NNOC's inaugural production of *Aida* in 1941. In 1934, Rhea was the first Black performer to be offered an opportunity to audition for the Metropolitan Opera, although the Met didn't hire its first Black soprano until 1955, when Marian Anderson received the honor. *Library of Congress, Music Division, National Negro Opera Company Collection, Box 8/Folder 24.*

performers denied access because of racist beliefs, ignorance and laws. This was the spark that ignited the fire in her and led to the founding of the NNOC in 1941.

The NNOC soon outgrew its rehearsal space in East Liberty and needed a larger venue for its cast. They found it on the third floor of 7101 Apple Street in Homewood, which became its home for the next two years. The inaugural performance of the National Negro Opera Company was in October 1941, at the Syria Mosque in Pittsburgh. It was Verdi's *Aida*, the same opera Madame Dawson had produced to critical acclaim at the NANM annual conference. This performance, along with major productions of *Faust*, *La Traviata*, Verdi's *Il Trovatore*, *Carmen*, *The Ordering of Moses* and *Ouanga*, earned the NNOC a reputation as an elite training and networking group for classical musicians and vocalists of color. Due in part to their unparalleled talent and professionalism, the NNOC became the first independent opera company invited to perform at the Metropolitan Opera in 1955. These opportunities and performances opened

Soprano Lillian Evanti (1890–1967) was lauded for her performance in the 1943 NNOC staging of Verdi's *La Traviata*. The *Chicago Defender* noted, "Miss Evanti expressed a desire to see more of her race become interested in opera. She explained that *La Traviata* is offering her an opportunity to translate the role of Violetta in English, in order that a better understanding will be afforded those witnessing the performance." *Evan-Tibbs Collection, Anacostia Community Museum, Smithsonian Institution, Gift of the Estate of Thurlow E. Tibbs Jr.*

doors for many of the classically trained singers and musicians remembered today, such as La Julia Rhea, lyric soprano Lillian Evanti and baritone Robert McFerrin Sr. (father of Bobby McFerrin), just to name a few.

The National Negro Opera Company was the first of its kind to be founded, owned and operated by a woman. Prior to Mary Cardwell Dawson's entrance onto this stage, the majority of Black opera companies were led by white men. By nature of her gender and ethnicity, Madame Dawson created history. The work provided by the NNOC built capacity for talented singers and others; essential behind-the-scenes talent such as seamstresses, costume designers and photographers were able to showcase their work and make their mark on the opera scene because of the vision of Madame Dawson.

The house on Apple Street remained in the Harris family until the death of Ada B. Harris, Woogie's wife, in 1975. The woman in this mid-1960s Teenie Harris photo might be her. In 2020, the National Trust for Historic Preservation added the building to its annual list of America's 11 Most Endangered Historic Places, which gave new life to the house and national attention to preservation efforts. *Carnegie Museum of Art, Pittsburgh, Heinz Family Fund, Charles "Teenie" Harris Archive, 2001.35.14668.*

Her extraordinary accomplishments in founding the National Negro Opera Company and advocating for racial equality in opera have been recognized, appropriately, in a play filled with music, *The Passion of Mary Cardwell Dawson*. Written by Sandra Seaton with music by Carlos Simon, it debuted in 2021 at the Glimmerglass Festival in Cooperstown, New York. Closer to home, the Pittsburgh Opera honored her at its 2022 Maecenas gala with a long-overdue Renaissance Award.

As we look to the future, the former home of the National Negro Opera Company House is more than just a building. It represents success, hope and progress for many African Americans. Beyond its symbolic importance and the stories it can tell, the commanding presence of the house itself and the spirit it radiates are motivation and inspiration for the evolution of humanity.

Bibliography

Altman, Susan. *Encyclopedia of African-American Heritage*. New York: Facts on File, 1997.

Fletcher-Brown, Charlene J. "National Negro Opera Company (1941–1962)." Blackpast.org, 2014. www.blackpast.org/african-american-history/national-negro-opera-company-1941-1962.

HistoricPittsburgh.org. "Guide to the Mary Cardwell Dawson Papers, 1916–2001." Mary Cardwell Dawson Papers Repository. Collection MSS#440. Pittsburgh: Heinz History Center. historicpittsburgh.org/islandora/object/pitt%3AUS-QQS-mss440/viewer.

Miller, Cait. "Mary Cardwell Dawson: First Lady of Opera." Library of Congress, 2019. blogs.loc.gov/music/2019/03/mary-cardwell-dawson-first-lady-of-opera.

The National Opera House. www.nationaloperahouse.org.

Oshiro, Shana. "Restoring the National Negro Opera House in Honor of Mary Cardwell Dawson." Chorusconnection.com, 2021. blog.chorusconnection.com/restoring-the-national-negro-opera-house-in-honor-of-mary-cardwell-dawson.

Pittsburgh Music History. "Mary Cardwell Dawson: Pioneering Founder of the National Negro Opera Company Who Fought Discrimination in Opera." sites.google.com/site/pittsburghmusichistory/pittsburgh-music-story/classic/mary-cardwell-dawson.

Wikipedia. "Mary Cardwell Dawson." en.wikipedia.org/wiki/Mary_Cardwell_Dawson.

Chapter 8

AUGUST WILSON
AND THE AUTOMOBILE:
A PECULIAR RELATIONSHIP

by Laurence A. Glasco, Associate Professor, History Department,
University of Pittsburgh

On a Friday afternoon in the early 1970s, Kenneth Owens-El and his friend Nick Flournoy were sitting in My Brother's Place, a restaurant-bar on Wylie Avenue in Pittsburgh's Hill District. The place was packed with patrons out enjoying themselves at the end of the week. Kenneth noticed that one patron was not socializing. Rather, he was sitting by himself at the end of the bar, chain smoking and writing on a yellow legal pad. Kenneth said to his friend Nick, "I keep seeing this guy around in some of the spots, some of the clubs, some of the bars. He looks like he's got issues....He just looks different." Nick replied, "[T]hat's because he *is* different. He's a genius. That's August Wilson....One day you'll hear about him. He is no joke."[88] Nick was correct. Wilson was a genius. He was different. And lots of people would soon hear about him. Within a decade or so, August Wilson would be on his way to becoming one of the most acclaimed playwrights in the history of American theater.

Like many geniuses, Wilson had a number of idiosyncrasies. He preferred to write in noisy, public spots like My Brother's Place and Eddie's Restaurant rather than in the quiet of his own apartment. He was high-strung, nervous and fidgety, a chain smoker who lit his next cigarette with the dying embers of the previous one. He was fascinated with the life stories of old-timers, so much so that he started dressing like them. He was considered by many a bohemian,

a Beatnik who got by on low-paying jobs that let him concentrate on writing but sometimes left him unable to pay the rent. On occasion, he wrote while walking down the street, a practice that caused some to wonder if he was a "numbers writer" and others to wonder if he had psychological issues. In addition to these idiosyncrasies, Wilson had one more peculiarity: a preference for walking rather than riding. Wilson never owned a car, never drove a car, never even had a driver's license. Many of Wilson's other peculiarities waned over time but not his ambivalent relationship with the automobile.

That Wilson never drove was remarkable. Born in 1945, he grew up at a time when the automobile was cherished as a symbol of freedom and the good life. The rich archives of *Pittsburgh Courier* photographer Teenie Harris have many examples of the automobile's high regard by Black people.

During and after World War II, Pittsburgh's booming, war-related economy created a time of full employment, enabling an increasing number of Black people to own cars. For August's family, however, doing so was out of the question. Fred Kittel, August's father, was a baker and German-speaking immigrant. Fred suffered from alcoholism and made only modest contributions to the family's finances.[89] August's mother, Daisy

Top: Portrait of August Wilson. *Courtesy* Pittsburgh Post-Gazette.

Bottom: Kenneth Owens-El, political organizer and human rights activist. *Courtesy Laurence Glasco.*

Wilson, raised six children in a small, crowded apartment that lacked such amenities as hot running water and an indoor toilet. As a youngster, August possibly resented those who could afford cars. When a friend once asked him why he hadn't been around lately, he replied, "I used to throw stones at cars, and so my mom would bring me in all summer long…to keep an eye on me."[90]

In 1958, just as August was entering his teenage years, Daisy broke up with Fred, and the family moved from its crowded Bedford Avenue

August Wilson and Nick Flournoy, friend, fellow poet and social activist. They were photographed in January 1989 on the occasion of Wilson being proclaimed Pittsburgh's "Man of the Year." *Courtesy Frank Hightower.*

Professional photographer Teenie Harris composed many images showing the high regard Black Pittsburghers had for fine automobiles. *Charles "Teenie" Harris Archive/Carnegie Museum of Art via Getty Images.*

apartment into a pleasant duplex on Flowers Avenue in Hazelwood. The move was possible because a new man had entered the family's life. David Bedford had a steady job, a decent salary and a generous disposition. Bedford also had an automobile: a late-model, light blue Cadillac in immaculate condition.

Dave taught Daisy to drive and gave her free use of the car. In return, she and the children took good care of the car, washing it almost every day in order to remove the coating of caustic ash deposited continually by the nearby Jones & Laughlin steel mill. To the astonishment of friends and neighbors—and a harbinger of idiosyncrasies to come—August washed the car barefoot, even on cold wintry days.[91]

The car allowed Daisy to get out of the city. Doing so was important, for having spent her childhood in the beautiful, heavily wooded mountains of western North Carolina, Daisy loved nature. Accordingly, Daisy and her girlfriend Julia Burley would drive over to Ohio and visit with Julia's relatives, who lived in the countryside outside Warren, not far from Youngstown. Daisy loved walking through the family's garden, admiring the flowers and vegetables.[92] On a few occasions, Daisy took the car on longer trips. In 1964, for example, she drove Dave—whose diabetes by then forced him to use a wheelchair—to New York City to see the newly opened World's Fair. A highlight of the visit was the chance to visit with her daughter Barbara and sister Faye.[93]

For Daisy, the Cadillac was a source of delight. But on one dreadful occasion, the car brought pain and shock. August and his mother had been on the outs ever since he dropped out of high school while still in the ninth grade. Tensions with his mother escalated to the point that, in 1962, August left home and joined the army. One day, while home on leave, he sought to impress his friends by letting them ogle the family's car, a new 1961 Cadillac with fishtails and black leather seats.[94] The friends were mightily impressed and asked August if they could take the car out for a spin. Without asking his mother's permission—and, no doubt, to his eternal regret—August agreed.[95]

Ronnie Culpepper was appointed driver because he was the only one with experience behind the wheel. It turned out to be not enough experience. While driving down Browns Hill Road toward Homestead, Ronnie had a head-on collision with another vehicle. The collision totaled the car, ejected the boys and knocked them temporarily unconscious. No one was seriously injured, but everyone knew that August would be in serious trouble. "We thought they were gonna kill [him]," said Earl Horsley, a friend and one of

Wilson's newly remodeled childhood residence, 1727 Bedford Avenue, 2022. *Courtesy Laurence Glasco.*

Top: In 1958, August Wilson's immediate family, along with David Bedford, his de facto stepfather, moved into this duplex at 185 Flowers Avenue, Hazelwood. *Courtesy Laurence Glasco.*

Bottom: David Bedford owned a light blue 1958 Cadillac like this one. Not included in the exhibit. *Photo, VDWI Automotive/ Alamy Stock. n.d. 1958 Cadillac Sedan De Ville classic car.*

the passengers. "That was their precious Cadillac....I didn't go anywhere near [their] house after that."[96]

The car accident might explain why August never owned an automobile, never operated one and seldom even rode in one. When he wanted a ride, he would ask friends or take public transportation. On Sundays, he and his girlfriend, Helen Lorraine Jackson of Homewood, would purchase bus tickets and spend the day riding around the city.[97] Usually, August got around by walking, something he had done for years. When he dropped out of school while still in the ninth grade, he didn't tell his mother. Rather, he secretly walked three miles every school day to the Carnegie Library in Oakland, where he would read to his heart's content. After heavy snowstorms, he and

Top: Portrait of David Bedford, 1951, companion of August Wilson's mother and owner of an attractive Cadillac. *Record Group#10/Governor Robert P. Casey/series # 10.3/courtesy of Pennsylvania Historical and Museum Commission, Pennsylvania State Archives.*

Bottom: Julia Burley and August Wilson. "Aunt Julie" was Wilson's childhood neighbor and close friend of his mother, Daisy. *Courtesy of the Burley family.*

his friend Earl Horsley earned money by walking two miles to Squirrel Hill, where they shoveled snow, sometimes until midnight.[98]

At the age of twenty, August left home, got an apartment and officially declared himself a poet. To acquire material to write about, he began walking the Hill, somewhat like an ethnographer or a flaneur in nineteenth-century Paris. Walking along Centre Avenue, the Hill's main commercial corridor, gave him the chance to learn by observing as he visited bars, diners and other places. He loved chatting with old-timers who gathered at Pat's Place, a combination newsstand, billiards parlor and cigar store.[99] And he spent many hours at Eddie's Restaurant smoking cigarettes and drinking endless cups of coffee while writing on a yellow legal pad and listening in on conversations that swirled around him. Walking let August observe daily life in ways that would not have been possible if he were driving.

Distance was of little concern. After moving to East Liberty, August regularly tramped two miles to the Kuntu Writers Workshop, held on Saturdays in Oakland at the University of Pittsburgh's Black Studies Department. As he told a friend, "I walked and I said that's okay because when I get there, I can get fifty cents from [my friend Rob Penny] and…get me some cigarettes. And Rob will give me a ride home, and I'm cool, man. That's all I needed. That's all I wanted."[100]

August had a photographic memory that let him recall in great detail things

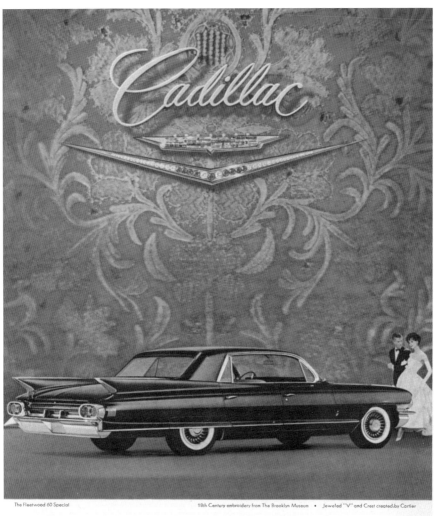

The Fleetwood 60 Special · 18th Century embroidery from The Brooklyn Museum · Jeweled "V" and Crest created by Cartier

The highest praise that can be accorded any product in any field is to declare it the Cadillac of its kind.

CADILLAC MOTOR CAR DIVISION, GENERAL MOTORS CORPORATION

he had seen and overheard during his walks. Once while ambling along Centre Avenue, he and his girlfriend overheard a heated exchange between a father and son. Pained and exasperated, the boy asked plaintively, "How come you ain't never liked me?" The father replied angrily, "Who the hell say I got to like you?...I put food on your table. I put clothes on your back.

Opposite: 1961 Cadillac. *Courtesy of AACA Library & Research Center, Hershey, Pennsylvania.*

Right: Earl Horsley, Wilson's friend and next-door neighbor in Hazelwood. *Courtesy Sonya Miles.*

Below: Pat's Place, a popular Wylie Avenue newsstand and tobacco store where Wilson spent time listening to old men talking and recounting their lives. *Carnegie Museum of Art, Pittsburgh, Charles "Teenie" Harris Archive, 2001.35.11334.*

Eddie's Restaurant, a popular Wylie Avenue eatery where August spent many hours smoking, drinking coffee and writing. *Charles "Teenie" Harris/ Carnegie Museum of Art via Getty Images.*

Left to right: Rob Penny, Ewarri Ellis and August Wilson, on occasion of Wilson's return to Pittsburgh in December 1989, when the city named him Man of the Year. Penny was a longtime friend of Wilson's and a leading poet and playwright. Ellis was director of the Halfway Art Gallery, where Wilson used to read poetry. *Courtesy Frank Hightower.*

Maisha Baton. Baton—poet, literary activist and good friend of August Wilson—drove August and others to literary events around town. *Courtesy Frank Hightower, 1989.*

[I do that] not because I like you but because it's my responsibility! You understand that?" Years later, August transformed that real-life exchange into a memorable scene in the play *Fences*.[101]

When necessary, August would ride with others, but he disliked riding with distracted drivers. This was the case with his sometime girlfriend Maisha Baton, who owned a car that she made available for driving others around. One snowy night, while bringing August and his good friend Claude Purdy back from a poetry reading, Maisha suddenly slammed on the brakes, turned around and said to the two men in the back, "I must not be a poet. I don't sound like them. Something's wrong." Claude surveyed the deep snow outside and exhorted, "We'll talk about it later!" But Maisha wanted to talk then and there. As she did so, the car rolled into a snowbank. "Keep going! Keep going!" the men pleaded. Maisha still laughs about that evening. "I'll never forget those guys shouting and trying to make me get out of that snow!"[102]

If automobiles made August nervous, flying terrified him. In 1978, shortly before turning thirty-three, he moved to St. Paul, Minnesota, in an effort to relaunch his career as a playwright. On his way to the airport, he stopped by Maisha's place and asked for some valium to calm his nerves.[103]

Although August did not embrace the automobile personally, he appreciated its social and psychological importance. This was reinforced once when he overheard a shooting victim ask someone for a ride to the hospital. For reasons both edifying and humorous, the car's owner said emphatically, "You ain't gon' get all that blood in *my* car!"[104]

In recognition of the automobile's social importance and widespread appeal, August's first major play featured jitneys, the name that locals gave to unlicensed "gypsy" cabs that provided transportation, jobs and business opportunities in Black neighborhoods that taxis often refused to

Outstanding actor Claude Purdy was a good friend and supporter of August Wilson. *Courtesy Jacqui Shoholm.*

service. August titled the play *Jitney* and set it in a station similar to one on Wylie Avenue that he and his friend Sala Udin used to frequent. During those visits, August would watch the drivers and listen as they bantered, played checkers and groused about how urban renewal would mean the end of both their neighborhood and their livelihoods. The set includes the real-life station's telephone number, as well as a blackboard with such essential information as the rates for going to different parts of the city, the day's policy "numbers" and the operating rules, as laid out by Jim Becker, the owner: "1. No overcharging; 2. Keep car clean; 3. No drinking; 4. Be courteous; 5. Replace and clean tools." In 1982, when *Jitney* premiered in Pittsburgh, it attracted large audiences of Black residents thrilled to watch a drama about an institution they had relied on for generations.[105]

Wilson's last play, *Radio Golf*, written in 2005 just before his death, touches on the automobile's emotional and psychological significance. Harmond Wilks, an ambitious businessman and aspiring politician, reminds his wife that he fell in love with her when, on their way to an event she had planned, his car blew a tire. "There you were," he tells her, "all dressed up. You didn't sit in the car. You were standing out along the road beside me....You didn't get mad. You didn't blame me. We worked through it together. I still

Westbrook Jitney Station. Now located on Centre Avenue, but originally situated on the corner of Wylie Avenue and Erin Street, Westbrook's bore the same telephone number as the station featured in Wilson's play *Jitney*. *Courtesy Laurence Glasco.*

Jitney, staged in 2010 by Pittsburgh Playwright's Theatre. On the left is Sala Udin as station owner Becker. To the right is Jonathan Berry, playing Becker's estranged son Booster. *Courtesy Mark Southers.*

Above: Published in 2005, *Radio Golf* is the tenth and final installment of August Wilson's Century Cycle. The play debuted on Broadway in 2007. *© 2022 Romare Bearden Foundation/Licensed by VAGA at Artists Rights Society (ARS), NY.*

Left: Wilson in front of his childhood home, 1727 Bedford Avenue in the Hill District. *Courtesy* Pittsburgh Post-Gazette.

remember you standing out there holding out your hands ready to take the rusty bolts. That's when I knew that I loved you." One can only wonder whether that bit of dialogue reflects the way August wished his mother, years earlier, had reacted to him wrecking the family car.

In the play, Harmond's friend Roosevelt Hicks regards automobiles and golf as manifestations of the good life. While driving around town, Hicks keeps a set of golf clubs in the trunk so as never to miss a chance to play a round. Hicks's character is based partly on August's friend Nick Flournoy, an erudite poet, elegant dresser and bon vivant who was famous for driving around the Hill with the top down and classical music blaring from the speakers. Flournoy, like Hicks, kept a set of clubs in his car trunk so as not to miss a game of golf should the opportunity come up.[106]

So there it is. On a professional level, Wilson depicted the automobile as an essential, cherished part of Black life. However, on a personal level, walking was what introduced Wilson to everyday Black life. That he appreciated the automobile's importance to others is a sign of his genius and of his unusual relationship with that icon of American life.

ANNOTATED BIBLIOGRAPHY

There is a large body of literature on Wilson's plays but surprisingly little about the author himself. Material for this essay is drawn largely from my forthcoming book manuscript "The Power of Place: August Wilson and Pittsburgh." For a brief treatment of Wilson and the Hill District, see Laurence Glasco and Christopher Rawson, *August Wilson: Pittsburgh Places in His Life and Plays*. Perhaps Wilson's own words are the best source for insights into his life. See *Conversations with August Wilson*, edited by Jackson R. Bryer and Mary C. Hartig. Mark Whitaker's recent book *Smoketown: The Untold Story of the Other Great Black Renaissance* contains an engaging, highly readable chapter on Wilson's Pittsburgh years. Also recommended are John Lahr, "Been Here and Gone: How August Wilson Brought a Century of Black American Culture to the Stage," *New Yorker Magazine*, April 16, 2001; and Marilyn Elkins, "Wilson, August," in William L. Andrews, et al., eds., *The Concise Oxford Companion to African American Literature* (available online). Finally, Teenie Harris's seventy thousand or so photographs of life in Black Pittsburgh can be seen online at cmoa.org/art/teenie-harris-archive.

APPENDIX

Page 120: The Crawford-Roberts neighborhood makes up the lower and middle sections of Pittsburgh's Historic Hill District. August Wilson used the neighborhood for the setting of many of his plays that were set in Pittsburgh.

Page 121: August Wilson spent part of his youth in Hazelwood after relocating there with his mother and siblings. Located in the southeastern section of Pittsburgh, Hazelwood was once home to many steelworkers, as the Hazelwood Coke Works once made its home there.

Pages 122–123: Situated on the banks of the Monongahela River, the boroughs of Rankin and Swissvale were home to many African Americans who migrated to Pittsburgh to seek work in the steel industry.

Page 124: A predominantly white neighborhood in northeastern Pittsburgh until the 1970s, Lincoln-Lemington-Belmar was home to William "Woogie" Harris and the National Negro Opera House.

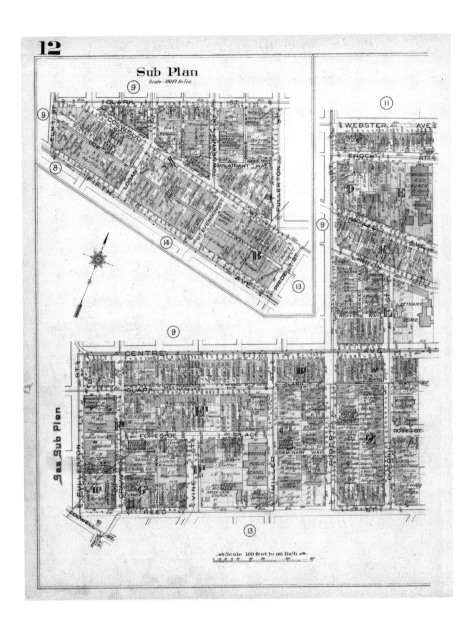

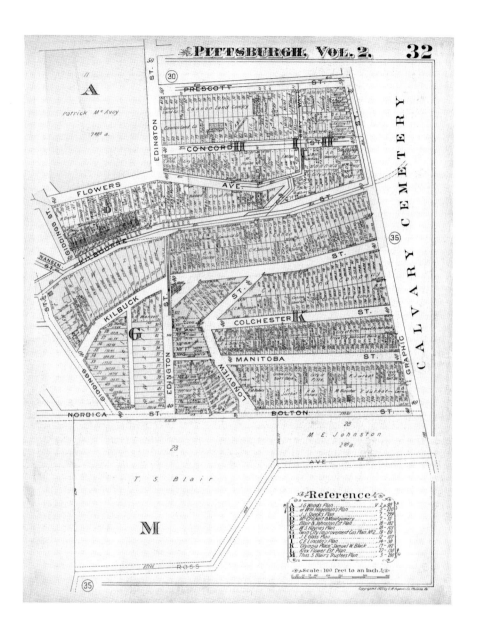

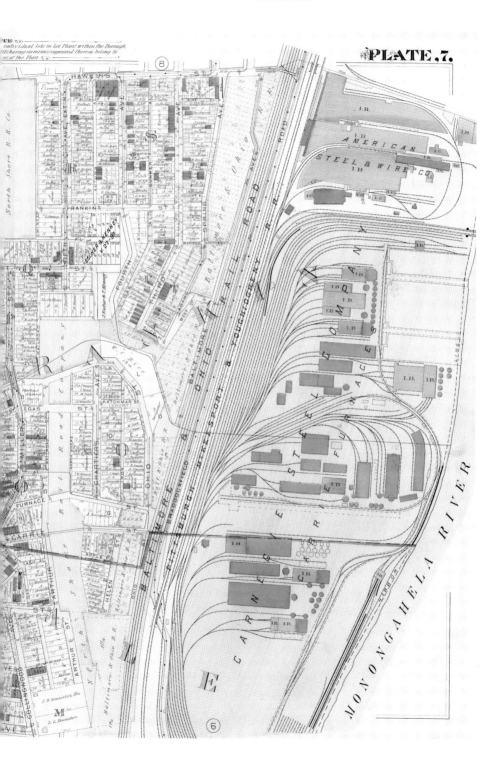

NOTES

Chapter 1

1. Austin Steward, *Twenty-Two Years a Slave and Forty Years a Freeman* (Canandaigua, NY: published by the author, 1867), 27.
2. "Popular Restauranteur to Move into Fine New Quarters Soon," *Pittsburgh Courier*, March 1, 1930, 8; "Dearing's Restaurant," display advertisement, *Pittsburgh Courier*, July 2, 1932, 6.
3. Post-Gazette.com, "The Story of Urban Renewal," old.post-gazette.com/businessnews/20000521eastliberty1.asp#:~:text=Urban%20redevelopment%2C%20the%20city's%20dominant,uprooted%20more%20than%205%2C000%20families.
4. Devin Rutan, "How Housing Policy Over the Last Century Has Made Pittsburgh What It Is Today," Public Source, www.publicsource.org/how-housing-policy-over-the-last-century-has-made-pittsburgh-what-it-is-today.
5. "Keystone Cities Lead All Others in Opportunity," *Pittsburgh Courier*, November 17, 1923, 13.

Chapter 2

6. Dennis Dickerson, "Black Steelworkers in Western Pennsylvania," *Pennsylvania Heritage Magazine*, Pennsylvania Historic and Museum Commission (December 1977).

7. Great Migration Project, "The Great Migration: A City Transformed (1916–1930), Historical Overview," Scribe Video Center, 2010, greatmigrationphl.org/node/24.

8. Cheryl Finley, Laurence Admiral Glasco and Joe William Trotter, "Harris, History and the Hill: Black Pittsburgh in the Twentieth Century," in *Teenie Harris, Photographer: Image, Memory, History* (Pittsburgh: University of Pittsburgh Press, 2011), 23–38.

9. Fon L. Gordon, "Driving 'Jim Crow': Cars and Race in the United States," Society for the History of Technology, *Technology's Stories* 8, no. 2 (September 28, 2020), www.technologystories.org/driving-jim-crow.

10. Jonathan Lanning, "How Ford Motors Equal Pay Policies Reduced Overall Labor Market Discrimination," Federal Reserve Bank of Chicago, *ProfitWise News and Views* no. 1 (August 2021), www.chicagofed.org/publications/profitwise-news-and-views/2021/ford-motor-equal-pay-policies.

11. Claude Johnson, "Negro Wages in 1910s, Compared to Money Opportunities Playing Basketball," Black Fives Foundation, August 6, 2008, www.blackfives.org/negro-wages-in-1910s-compared-to-money-opportunities-playing-basketball.

12. Jim Koscs, "How Nicholas Dreystadt Ended Racism at Cadillac in the 1930s—or Tried To," *Hagerty*, October 22, 2019, www.hagerty.com/media/automotive-history/nicholas-dreystadt-ended-racism-at-cadillac-in-the-1930s.

13. Detroit Historical Society, "Encyclopedia of Detroit," detroithistorical.org/learn/encyclopedia-of-detroit/davis-edward.

14. Gretchen Sullivan Sorin, *Driving While Black: African American Travel and the Road to Civil Rights* (New York: Liveright Publishing, 2020).

15. James W. Loewen, *Sundown Towns: A Hidden Dimension of American Racism* (New York: New Press, 2018).

16. Audrey Thomas, "Recreation without Humiliation: The Preservation of Travel Guide Resources in Portsmouth, Virginia," master's thesis, University of Georgia, 2018, getd.libs.uga.edu/pdfs/thomas_audrey_e_201805_mhp.pdf.

17. August Meier and Elliott Rudwick, 1969, "The Boycott Movement against Jim Crow Streetcars in the South, 1900–1906," *Journal of American History* 55, no. 4 (March 1969): 756, doi.org/10.2307/1900151.

18. Laura Scott Grantmyre, "Conflicting Visual Representations of Redevelopment in Pittsburgh's Hill District, 1943–1968," master's thesis, University of Pittsburgh, 2013, dscholarship.pitt.edu/20304/1/ETD_GRANTMYRE_12_15.pdf.

19. Richard J. Lundman and Robert L. Kaufman, "Driving While Black: Effects of Race, Ethnicity, and Gender on Citizen Self-Reports of Traffic Stops and Police Actions," *Criminology* 41, no. 1 (2003): 195–220, doi.org/10.1111/j.1745-9125.2003.tb00986.x.

Chapter 3

20. Edwin Nathaniel Harleston, *The Toiler's Life* (Philadelphia: Jensen Press, 1907).
21. Andrew Buni, *Robert L. Vann and the* Pittsburgh Courier*: Politics and Black Journalism* (Pittsburgh: University of Pittsburgh Press, 1974), 43.
22. Pittsburgh Directory, 1909, R.L. Polk & Co. and R.L. Dudley, Publishers, page 645; Pittsburgh, Pennsylvania, City Directory, 1910, R.L. Polk & Co. and R.L. Dudley, publishers, p. 1059; 1910 census Place: Pittsburgh Ward 4, Allegheny, Pennsylvania; Roll: T624_1300; Page 11A; Enumeration District: 322; Image: 255.
23. Samuel W. Black, "America's Best Weekly: One Hundred Years of the *Pittsburgh Courier*," *Western Pennsylvania History Magazine* (Spring 2010): 24.
24. Buni, *Robert L. Vann*, 19.
25. Black, "America's Best Weekly," 23.
26. Samuel W. Black, "The Negro Migrant to Pittsburgh: A Review of the Conditions 100 Years Ago," *Western Pennsylvania History Magazine* (Winter 2017–18): 39.
27. Laurance Glasco, "Double Burden: The Black Experience in Pittsburgh," in *African Americans in Pennsylvania: Shifting Historical Perspectives*, edited by Joe William Trotter and Eric Ledell Smith (University Park: Pennsylvania State University Press, 1997), 418.
28. Peter Gottlieb, *Making Their Own Way: Southern Blacks' Migration to 1916–30* (Urbana: University of Illinois Press, 1997), 65.
29. Heinz History Center, exhibition label, "America's Best Weekly: A Century of the *Pittsburgh Courier*," May 2010–May 2011.
30. "Wealth of 681 Negroes," *Pittsburgh Courier*, January 6, 1912, 4.
31. Joe William Trotter and Jared Day, *Race and Renaissance: African Americans in Pittsburgh Since World War II* (Pittsburgh: University of Pittsburgh Press, 2010), 13.
32. Ervin Dyer, "Revisiting the Great Migration," *Pittsburgh Post-Gazette*, February 25, 2001.
33. "Voting Without Terror," *Pittsburgh Courier*, November 6, 1948, 16.

34. "The Way to Stop Migration," *Pittsburgh Courier*, August 4, 1923, 8.

35. "GOP Is Flayed by Vann," *Pittsburgh Courier*, September 17, 1932, 1.

36. Abraham Epstein, *The Negro Migrant in Pittsburgh* (Pittsburgh: University of Pittsburgh School of Economics, 1918), 3; Samuel W. Black, "The Negro Migrant in Pittsburgh: A Review of the Conditions 100 Years Ago," *Western Pennsylvania History Magazine* (Winter 2017–18): 40.

37. Trotter and Day, *Race and Renaissance*, 7, 13. Trotter cited the work of Dennis Dickerson and provided further clarity on the history of Black steelworkers in western Pennsylvania.

38. Trotter and Day, *Race and Renaissance*, 7.

39. Emmett J. Scott, *Negro Migration During the War* (Washington, D.C.: Carnegie Endowment for International Peace, 1920), 14.

40. Trotter and Day, *Race and Renaissance*, 46.

Chapter 4

41. John L. Clark, *Pittsburgh Courier*, February 20, 1926, 8.

42. The first major voluntary migration of African Americans (approximately forty thousand people) from the South after the American Civil War was into Kansas, Oklahoma and Colorado and is known as the "Exoduster Movement of 1879." However, the next great migration—which ultimately involved some six million people—is what has become known as the Great Migration. The first phase took place from 1910 to 1940, the second from 1940 to 1980.

43. *Pittsburgh Courier*, April 3, 1926, 3.

44. Jackleg definition: *Noun*—an unskilled or unscrupulous itinerant worker or practitioner (www.dictionary.com). The definition of jackleg as an adjective is found in the Oxford English Dictionary (OED): "Incompetent, unskilled; unscrupulous, dishonest. Frequently used of lawyers and preachers." The OED pegs the term as a U.S. invention and dates its first appearance in print to 1850 (www.word-detective. com/2012/01/jackleg).

45. William Attaway, *Blood on the Forge* (New York: New York Review of Books, 1941).

46. Herbert Edwards, interview by Ron Baraff and Julie Throckmorton, April 29, 2003, transcript, Steel Industry Heritage Corporation, Rivers of Steel Archives, Pittsburgh, Pennsylvania.

47. John Hughey, interview by Doris Dyen, September 8, 1989, transcript, Steel Industry Heritage Task Force, Rivers of Steel Archives, Pittsburgh, Pennsylvania.

48. Emergency Immigration Act of 1921, the Immigration Restriction Act of 1921, the Per Centum Law and the Johnson Quota Act (Ch. 8, 42 Stat. 5 of May 19, 1921) were formulated mainly in response to the large influx of southern and eastern Europeans and successfully restricted their immigration, as well as that of other "undesirables," to the United States. Although intended as temporary legislation, it "proved, in the long run, the most important turning-point in American immigration policy" because it added two new features to American immigration law: numerical limits on immigration and the use of a quota system for establishing those limits, which came to be known as the National Origins Formula.

49. *Pittsburgh Courier*, July 2, 1927, 3.

50. Interchurch World Movement of North America, Bureau of Industrial Research, *Report on the Steel Strike of 1919* (New York: Harcourt, Brace and Howe, 1920).

51. Edwards interview.

52. The consent decrees were signed in 1974 by nine steel companies and the United Steelworkers of America on the same day the Equal Employment Opportunity Commission and the secretary of labor filed suit against the companies and the union. The suit charged "massive patterns and practices of hiring and job assignment discrimination on the bases of race, sex and national origin," the Circuit Court noted. Several groups, including the National Organization for Women, appealed the agreement. But the court ruled that the groups could not intervene in the case. Under a consent decree, the defendants agreed to stop the practices that led to the suit. The nine companies that signed the decree were Allegheny-Ludlum Industries, Inc., Armco Steel Corporation, Bethlehem Steel Corporation, Jones & Laughlin Steel Corporation, National Steel Corporation, Republic Steel Corporation, United States Steel Corporation, Wheeling-Pittsburgh Steel Corporation and Youngstown Sheet and Tube Company. The second decree deals mainly with company-controlled issues not subject to collective bargaining (*New York Times*, August 19, 1975, 4).

53. Archie Coles, interview by Tiffani Emig, July 13, 2009, transcript, Steel Industry Heritage Corporation/Rivers of Steel, Rivers of Steel Archives, Pittsburgh, Pennsylvania.

54. Hughey interview.

Chapter 5

55. Earl Lewis, *In Their Own Interest: Race, Class, and Power in Twentieth Century Norfolk, Virginia* (Berkeley: University of California Press, 1991), 90–96.

56. Dennis Dickerson, *Out of the Crucible: Black Steelworkers in Western Pennsylvania, 1875–1980* (Albany: State University of New York Press, 1986), 37–40, quote, 37.

57. Laurence A. Glasco, *The WPA History of the Negro in Pittsburgh* (Pittsburgh: University of Pittsburgh Press, 2004), 347.

58. Peter Gottlieb, *Making Their Own Way: Southern Blacks' Migration to Pittsburgh, 1916–30* (Urbana: University of Illinois Press, 1987), 74–75.

59. Joe William Trotter Jr., *Workers on Arrival: Black Labor in the Making of America* (Oakland: University of California Press, 2019), 78.

60. Gottlieb, *Making Their Own Way*, 49.

61. John A. Fitch, *The Steel Workers* (1910; report. University of Pittsburgh Press, 1989), 29.

62. Dickerson, *Out of the Crucible*, 124.

63. Ibid., 61.

64. Jacqueline Jones, *Labor of Love, Labor of Sorrow: Black Women, Work, and the Family from Slavery to the Present* (New York: Basic Books, 1985), 167–68; Gottlieb, *Making Their Own Way*, 107.

65. Quotes in Horace R. Cayton and George S. Mitchell, *Black Workers and the New Unions* (Chapel Hill: University of North Carolina Press, 1939), excerpt, in John H. Bracey, August Meier and Elliott Rudwick, eds., *Black Workers and Organized Labor* (Belmont, CA: Wadsworth Publishing Company, 1971), 135; Bruce Nelson, *Divided We Stand: American Workers and the Struggle for Black Equality* (Princeton, NJ: Princeton University Press, 2001), 167; Linda Nyden, "Black Miners in Western Pennsylvania, 1925–1931: The National Miners Union and the United Mine Workers of America," *Science and Society* 41, no. 1 (Spring 1977): 86.

66. Joe William Trotter Jr., *River Jordan: African American Urban Life in the Ohio Valley* (Lexington: University Press of Kentucky, 1998), 107.

67. Gottlieb, *Making Their Own Way*, 75–76; Joe William Trotter Jr. and Jared Day, *Race and Renaissance: African Americans in Pittsburgh since World War II* (Pittsburgh: University of Pittsburgh Press), 12–13.

68. Andrew Buni, *Robert L. Vann of the* Pittsburgh Courier*: Politics and Black Journalism* (Pittsburgh: University of Pittsburgh Press, 1974), 62–63; John Bodnar, Roger Simon and Michael P. Weber, *Lives of Their Own: Blacks,*

Italians, and Poles in Pittsburgh, 1900–1960 (Urbana: University of Illinois Press, 1982), 159, 179.

69. Trotter and Day, *Race and Renaissance*, 13–14.

70. Steve Mellon and Tony Norman, "The Notorious Trial of Joe Thomas," *Pittsburgh Post-Gazette*, September 23, 2019.

71. Mellon, *Post-Gazette*.

72. Mark Whitaker, *Smoketown: The Untold Story of the Other Great Black Renaissance* (New York: Simon and Schuster, 2018); Joe William Trotter Jr., *Pittsburgh and the Urban League Movement: A Century of Social Service and Activism* (Lexington: University Press of Kentucky, 2020).

Chapter 6

73. Chester A. Washington, "Sportively Speaking," *Pittsburgh Courier*, May 7, 1932; "Hubbard Pitches Three-Hit Game to Beat Paige, 1 to 0," *Pittsburgh Courier*, May 7, 1932; Mark Ribowsky, *The Power and the Darkness: The Life of Josh Gibson in the Shadows of the Game* (New York: Simon and Schuster, 1996), 91.

74. Brian McKenna, "Gus Greenlee," Society for American Baseball Research, sabr.org/bioproj/person/gus-greenlee.

75. "Gus Greenlee (Big Mogul of Pittsburgh)," *Pittsburgh Courier*, November 19, 1932.

76. John N. Ingham and Lynne B. Feldman, *African-American Business Leaders: A Biographical Dictionary* (Westport, CT: Greenwood Press, 1994), 293–307.

77. Isabel Wilkerson, "The Long-Lasting Legacy of the Great Migration," Smithsonian, September 2016, www.smithsonianmag.com/history/long-lasting-legacy-great-migration-180960118.

78. Ingham and Feldman, *African-American Business Leaders*, 293–307; Rob Ruck, *Sandlot Seasons: Sport in Black Pittsburgh* (Urbana: University of Illinois Press, 1993), 138–41; "Gambling and Clubs Are Also Under Ban," *Pittsburgh Daily Post*, March 25, 1925.

79. Ruck, *Sandlot Seasons*, 146; "Numbers Racket Menaces Hill Real Estate Values," *Pittsburgh Post-Gazette*, September 26, 1930.

80. Laurence Glasco, "An American Life, and American Story: Charles 'Teenie' Harris and Images of Black Pittsburgh," in Cherly Finley, Laurence Glasco and Joe W. Trotter, *Teenie Harris, Photographer: Image, Memory, History* (Pittsburgh: University of Pittsburgh Press, 2011), 1–22; Lulu Lippincott, "Riding in the Family Car with Teenie Harris,"

Storyboard, Carnegie Museum of Art, storyboard.cmoa.org/2015/12/riding-in-the-family-car-with-teenie-harris.

81. "Fields Afire as Dry Spell, Heat Continue," *Pittsburgh Post-Gazette*, August 4, 1930; Ruck, *Sandlot Seasons*, 144–45.

82. "Gus Greenlee (Big Mogul of Pittsburgh)," *Pittsburgh Courier*, November 19, 1932; "Gus Greenlee: Owner of the Legendary Crawford Grill and the Pittsburgh Crawfords," Pittsburgh Music History, sites.google.com/site/pittsburghmusichistory/pittsburgh-music-story/managers-and-promoters/gus-greenlee; Ribowsky, *The Power and the Darkness*, 76.

83. Jim Bankes, *The Pittsburgh Crawfords* (Jefferson, NC: McFarland, 2001), 3–17; Ruck, *Sandlot Seasons*, 152–53; Larry Tye, *Satchel: The Life and Times of an American Legend* (New York: Random House, 2009), 51–58.

84. Bankes, *Pittsburgh Crawfords*, 22; "Crawfords Basking in Sun's Spotlight," *Pittsburgh Courier*, April 2, 1932.

85. John L. Clark, "The Rise and Fall of Greenlee Field," *Pittsburgh Courier*, December 10, 1938; "Ches Sez," *Pittsburgh Courier*, January 2, 1937; "Grays Get Gibson," *Pittsburgh Courier*, March 27, 1937.

86. "Writer Calls East-West Tilt Most Colorful in Sports History," *Pittsburgh Courier*, September 8, 1934; "Smitty's Sports Spurts," *Pittsburgh Courier*, April 28, 1945.

87. "Wendell Smith's Sport Beat," *Pittsburgh Courier*, July 19, 1952.

Chapter 8

88. Kenneth Owens-El, interview by the author, July 13, 2017, May 7, 2022.

89. August was named Fred Kittel after his father and was known as Freddy Kittel to family, old friends and neighbors. At the age of twenty, when he declared himself a poet, he chose August Wilson as a pen name.

90. Jerry Rhodes, interview by the author, January 17, 2016.

91. Marva Scott-Starks, Daisy's neighbor, thinks the family washed the car every other day; Earl Horsley, another neighbor, interview by the author, May 14, 2013.

92. Julia Burley, interview by the author, October 3, 2012.

93. Barbara Wilson, interview by the author, n.d.

94. *Fishtail* may be a regional name for tailfin.

95. Earl Horsley, interview by the author, May 14, 2013.

96. Ibid.

97. Ibid.

98. Ibid.

99. Chip Brown, "The Light in August," *Esquire* (April 1989), 123.

100. August Wilson, interview by Lee Kiburi, April 6, 1999.

101. Franki Williams, several informal conversations with the author, 2015.

102. Maisha Baton, interview by Lee Kiburi, December 26, 2007.

103. Ibid.

104. John Lahr, "Been Here and Gone: How August Wilson Brought a Century of Black American Culture to the Stage," *New Yorker*, April 16, 2001, 15.

105. Diane R. Powell, "'Jitney' Captures Drama Behind Hill Substitute Taxi-Cab Service," *New Pittsburgh Courier*, November 20, 1982, 7.

106. Mike Flournoy, interview by the author, June 16, 2013; Gail Austin, interview by the author, June 21, 2013; Moses Carper, interview by the author, November 9, 2007; Sala din, interview by the author, June 7, 2013; August Wilson, interview by Lee Kiburi, April 6, 1999.

FURTHER READINGS

Altman, Susan. *Encyclopedia of African American Heritage*. New York: Facts on File, 1997.

Bodnar, John, Roger Simon and Michael P. Weber. *Lives of Their Own: Blacks, Italians, and Poles in Pittsburgh, 1900–1960*. Urbana: University of Illinois Press, 1982.

Branchik, Blaine J., and Judy Foster Davis. "Black Gold: A History of the African-American Elite Market Segment." *Charm*, 2007.

Dickerson, Dennis. 1977. "Black Steelworkers in Western Pennsylvania." *Pennsylvania Heritage Magazine*, December 1977. paheritage.wpengine.com/article/black-steelworkers-western-pennsylvania.

———. *Out of the Crucible: Black Steelworkers in Western Pennsylvania, 1875–1980*. Albany: State University of New York Press, 1986.

Epstein, Abraham. *The Negro Migrant in Pittsburgh*. Pittsburgh: University of Pittsburgh Press, 1918.

Finley, Cheryl, Laurence Admiral Glasco and Joe William Trotter. "Harris, History and the Hill: Black Pittsburgh in the Twentieth Century." In *Teenie Harris, Photographer: Image, Memory, History*. Pittsburgh: University of Pittsburgh Press, 2011.

Fletcher-Brown, Charlene J. "National Negro Opera Company (1941–1962)." Black Past, April 16, 2014. www.blackpast.org/african-american-history/national-negro-opera-company-1941-1962.

Glasco, Laurence. "Double Burden: The Black Experience in Pittsburgh." In *City at the Point: Essays on the Social History of Pittsburgh*, edited by Samuel P. Hays. Pittsburgh: University of Pittsburgh Press, 1989.

Gordon, Fon L. "Driving 'Jim Crow': Cars and Race in the United States." Technology's Stories 8, no. 2 (September 28, 2020). www.technologystories.org/driving-jim-crow.

Gottlieb, Peter. *Making Their Own Way: Southern Blacks' Migration to Pittsburgh, 1916–30.* Urbana: University of Illinois Press, 1987.

Grantmyre, Laura Scott. "Conflicting Visual Representations of Redevelopment in Pittsburgh's Hill District, 1943–1968." Master's thesis, University of Pittsburgh, 2013. dscholarship.pitt.edu/20304/1/ETD_GRANTMYRE_12_15.pdf.

The Great Migration—A City Transformed. "Historical Overview." Greatmigrationphl.org. 2010. greatmigrationphl.org/node/24.

Guide to the Mary Cardwell Dawson Papers, 1916–2001. Mary Cardwell Dawson Papers Repository, Heinz History Center Collection, MSS#440. historicpittsburgh.org/islandora/object/pitt%3AUS-QQS-mss440/viewer.

Henderson, Ryan. "John Hughey & the Legacy of Black Workers at the Carrie Furnaces." Rivers of Steel, February 18, 2021. riversofsteel.com/black-workers-at-carrie.

Johnson, Claude. 2008. "Negro Wages in 1910s, Compared to Money Opportunities Playing Basketball." The Black Fives Foundation, August 6, 2008. www.blackfives.org/negro-wages-in-1910s-compared-to-money-opportunities-playing-basketball.

Koscs, Jim. "How Nicholas Dreystadt Ended Racism at Cadillac in the 1930s—or Tried To." Hagerty, October 22, 2019. www.hagerty.com/media/automotive-history/nicholas-dreystadt-ended-racism-at-cadillac-in-the-1930s.

Lang, Jonathan. "How Ford Motor's Equal Pay Policies Reduced Overall Labor Market Discrimination." Federal Reserve Bank of Chicago. *ProfitWise News and Views*, no. 1 (August 2021). www.chicagofed.org/publications/profitwise-news-and-views/2021/ford-motor-equal-pay-policies.

Loewen, James W. *Sundown Towns: A Hidden Dimension of American Racism.* New York: New Press, 2018.

Lundman, Richard J., and Robert L. Kaufman. "Driving While Black: Effects of Race, Ethnicity, and Gender on Citizen Self-Reports of Traffic Stops and Police Actions." *Criminology* 41, no. 1 (2003): 195–220. doi.org/10.1111/j.1745-9125.2003.tb00986.x.

Macy, Xavier. "Drive toward Freedom: African American: The Story of Black Automobility in the Fight for Civil Rights." Master's theses, 2010–19. commons.lib.jmu.edu/master201019/72.

Massey, Douglas S., and Nancy A. Denton. *American Apartheid: Segregation and the Making of the Underclass*. Cambridge, MA: Harvard University Press, 1993.

Meier, August, and Elliott Rudwick. "The Boycott Movement against Jim Crow Streetcars in the South, 1900–1906." *Journal of American History* 55, no. 4 (1969): 756. doi.org/10.2307/1900151.

Mellon, Steve, and Tony Norman. "The Notorious Trial of Joe Thomas." *Pittsburgh Post-Gazette*, September 23, 2019.

Miller, Cait. "Mary Cardwell Dawson: First Lady of Opera." Library of Congress, March 1, 2019. blogs.loc.gov/music/2019/03/mary-cardwell-dawson-first-lady-of-opera.

MOMA. "Jacob Lawrence's Migration Series, Panel 38." www.moma.org/interactives/exhibitions/2015/onewayticket/panel/38.

National Opera House. www.nationaloperahouse.org.

Oshiro, Shana. "Restoring the National Negro Opera House in Honor of Mary Cardwell Dawson." Chorus Connection, March 29, 2021. blog.chorusconnection.com/restoring-the-national-negro-opera-house-in-honor-of-mary-cardwell-dawson#:~:text=Madame%20Dawson%27s%20success%20with%20her,from%20auditions%20within%20ten%20states.

Pittsburgh Music History. "Mary Cardwell Dawson, Pioneering Founder of the National Negro Opera Company Who Fought Discrimination in Opera." sites.google.com/site/pittsburghmusichistory/pittsburgh-music-story/classic/mary-cardwell-dawson.

Seiler, Cotton. *Republic of Drivers: A Cultural History of Automobility in America*. Chicago: University of Chicago Press, 2009.

Smith, Eric Ledell. *African Americans in Pennsylvania: Shifting Historical Perspectives*. College Park: Pennsylvania Historical and Museum Commission and the Pennsylvania State University Press, 1997.

Sorin, Gretchen Sullivan. *Driving while Black: African American Travel and the Road to Civil Rights*. New York: Liveright Publishing Corporation, a Division of W.W. Norton & Company, 2020.

Sugrue, Thomas. *Driving while Black: The Car and Race Relations in Modern America*. Automobile in American Life and Society, University of Michigan. www.autolife.umd.umich.edu/Race/R_Casestudy/R_Casestudy2.htm.

Taeuber, Karl E., and Alma F. Taeuber. *Negroes in Cities: Residential Segregation and Neighborhood Change*. Chicago: Aldine Publishing Company, 1965.

Thomas, Audrey. "Recreation without Humiliation: The Preservation of Travel Guide Resources in Portsmouth, Virginia." 2018. getd.libs.uga.edu/pdfs/thomas_audrey_e_201805_mhp.pdf.

Trotter, Joe William, Jr. *Pittsburgh and the Urban League Movement: A Century of Social Service and Activism.* Lexington: University of Kentucky Press, 2020.

———. *River Jordan: African American Urban Life in the Ohio Valley.* Lexington: University Press of Kentucky, 1998.

Trotter, Joe William, Jr., and Jared Day. *Race and Renaissance: African Americans in Pittsburgh since World War II.* Pittsburgh: University of Pittsburgh Press, 2010.

U.S. Department of Labor. "Legal Highlight: The Civil Rights Act of 1964." 2019. www.dol.gov/agencies/oasam/civil-rights-center/statutes/civil-rights-act-of-1964.

Wells, Christopher. "Grand Opera as Racial Uplift: The National Negro Opera Company, 1941–1962." *Pittsburgh Post-Gazette*, n.d.

ABOUT THE AUTHORS

RON BARAFF is a Pittsburgh native who has been in his current position as the director of historic resources and facilities for the Rivers of Steel National Heritage Area in Homestead, Pennsylvania, since 1998. He supervises the Rivers of Steel's Archives and Museum, Interpretive and Tourism Programming and Historic Sites. He has worked on a variety of public history projects, including many national and international television shows and documentaries.

SAMUEL W. BLACK is the director of the African American Program at the Senator John Heinz History Center. Black is the editor of *Soul Soldiers: African Americans and the Vietnam Era* (2006), coauthor of *Through the Lens of Allen E. Cole: A Photographic History of African Americans in Cleveland, Ohio* (2012) and editor of *The Civil War in Pennsylvania: The African American Experience* (2013). His administrative experience considers his serving on the Heinz History Center accreditation team and the development of its Museum of African American History initiative.

KIMBERLY CADY is the associate curator for the Car and Carriage Museum at the Frick Pittsburgh, where she cares for and develops exhibitions related to the organization's historic transportation collection. She has a BA in liberal studies from Mansfield University of Pennsylvania and an MA in museum studies from the University of Oklahoma. Prior to her work at the Frick, she served as the collections manager at the Pennsylvania State

Police Museum in Hershey and the assistant curator at the Tioga Point Museum in Athens, Pennsylvania.

LAURENCE GLASCO is an associate professor of history at the University of Pittsburgh, where he teaches and conducts research on race and caste in world perspective and on the history of Black Pittsburgh.

JONNET SOLOMON is the executive director of the National Opera House, a nonprofit organization working to restore and maintain a historic home in Pittsburgh, Pennsylvania. Educated in public schools and an avid volunteer, Solomon earned both volunteer and accounting scholarships and attended Duquesne University in Pittsburgh, earning a bachelor's degree in accounting. The drive to uncover, share, educate and preserve the rich history and legacy of the House on Apple Street, coupled with her own background as a musician, inspired Solomon and her friend Miriam White to lead the campaign to preserve the house and reconnect its history to the community.

GRETCHEN SULLIVAN SORIN is director and distinguished service professor at the Cooperstown Graduate Program, a training program for museum professionals that is part of the State University of New York at Oneonta. She is the author of *Driving while Black: African American Travel and the Road to Civil Rights*. The book was a finalist for the NAACP's Image Award for Outstanding Literary Work. Sorin is also the senior historian with filmmaker Ric Burns on the PBS documentary film *Driving while Black: Race, Space and Mobility*.

JOE WILLIAM TROTTER JR. is the Giant Eagle University Professor of History and Social Justice at Carnegie Mellon University and president of the Urban History Association.

MARK WHITAKER is the author of the critically acclaimed books *Smoketown: The Untold Story of the Other Great Black Renaissance* and *My Long Trip Home: A Family Memoir*. He is a contributor to *CBS Sunday Morning* and was previously the managing editor of CNN Worldwide and a reporter and editor at *Newsweek*, where he rose to become the first African American leader of a national newsweekly.

THE FRICK PITTSBURGH offers authentic experiences with art, history and nature that inspire and delight. Visitors of all ages and backgrounds are warmly welcomed to explore collections of fine and decorative arts, vehicles, historic objects and buildings—including Clayton, the Frick family home and only intact Gilded Age mansion remaining from Pittsburgh's Millionaire's Row—left as a legacy to the people of Pittsburgh by Helen Clay Frick, daughter of noted industrialist and art collector Henry Clay Frick. Alongside these treasures, the Frick offers an active schedule of temporary exhibitions and programs on its ten-acre garden campus in the heart of Pittsburgh's East End. Information about The Frick Pittsburgh is available online at TheFrickPittsburgh.org.